CHANGING PACE

Outdoor Games for Experiential Learning

Carmine M. Consalvo

HRD Press, Inc. & Lakewood Publications

in association with Gower Publishing, Ltd.

Published by HRD Press, Inc.
    22 Amherst Road
    Amherst, MA 01002
    800-822-2801
    (413) 253-3490 (fax)

Lakewood Publications
50 South Ninth Street
Minneapolis, MN 55402
800-707-7769

ISBN 0-87425-354-3

In association with
    Gower Publishing Ltd.
    Aldershot
    Hampshire
    England

Production Design by Page Design Services
Editorial Work by Lisa Wood
Cover Design by Steve Oringdulph

Contents

List of Figures

Preface

This book is designed to assist facilitators and trainers of human resource development in the use of outdoor games as a vehicle for learning. It contains sixty-three outdoor experiences that can be conducted easily and safely with a minimum of materials and preparation. Neither carpentry nor outdoor skills are necessary to conduct these games.

The **Introduction** offers a commentary on how and why the use of experiential games and fantasy in an outdoor context enhances training. Next, the **Trainer Guidelines** give practical training insights and suggestions for making effective use of the sixty-three outdoor games.

Each activity follows a standard format:

- Title.

- *Summary* — provides a brief but vivid picture of what the game requires the participants to do.

- *Objectives* — lists the primary training themes with which the game is concerned. Other secondary goals are possible. A reading of the *Commentary* section will often clarify the nature of the learning goals associated with the activity.

- *Materials* — lists any resources needed in order to set up the activity. Most are commonly available in a local hardware store or lumberyard.

- *Time Limit* — gives an approximate duration of the entire activity including the introduction, the challenge, and the review and discussion. The time is usually presented as a range, such as 45–75 minutes, with approximately 15 minutes allowed for the review. All things being equal, the middle of the range is the best estimate of the actual time needed.

- *Procedure* — details all the preparation in terms of what materials to put where, how, and why. The basic structure necessary for setting the stage for the game is described including logistical information and graphics as needed. A sequential method for presenting the game to the group follows. It includes guidelines for what to do, when, and how. Both the content and the process involved in each segment of the presentation are clarified.

- *Commentary* — explains the potential strengths and difficulties or pitfalls related to the game. Also indicated are what to watch for and fruitful lines of inquiry to pursue during the review based on prior experience with the activity. Safety considerations and preventive measures necessary to minimize the likelihood of mishaps are usually mentioned here.

- *Variations* — presents guidelines for alternative ways of conducting the activity. This section also lists other games that may be productively used in conjunction with the activity.

Please contact me with questions or concerns about an activity or to share adaptations or anecdotes. Send me your favorite game and I will credit you if I use it in the next volume.

Carmine M. Consalvo
WORKPLAY
RR 1 Box 1825
N. Ferrisburgh, VT 05473

Acknowledgments

A number of people, books, and organizations deserve credit for their contributions to these outdoor games. My wife Anna deserves special thanks. Her knowledge as an outdoor ropes course trainer, her careful reading of the manuscript, and in particular her understanding, patience, and encouragement have made this book a reality. My son Alex also deserves credit for showing remarkable restraint, for an eight-year-old, in not disturbing me while I wrote at home.

While most of the scenarios are my originals, the majority of the activities are variations of existing games. Keeping track of where I first came across what activity is difficult. The various books by Karl Rohnke of Project Adventure, Hamilton, Massachusetts are my main source of ideas for outdoor games. The following activities were inspired by games I first saw presented by specific trainers: **Gold Bricks** — Ric Timmons of Inspiring Adventure in Management, Bethel, Vermont; **Moon Walk** — Skip Dewhirst of Pine Ridge Adventure, Richmond, Vermont; and **Heroes, Heroines and Healers** — Andrea Van Liew of Pine Ridge Adventure, Richmond, Vermont. The following books and publications were primary sources of game ideas and inspiration: *Silver Bullets, The Bottomless Bag, Cowtails & Cobras, The Bottomless Baggie,* and the newsletter "Bag of Tricks" by Karl Rohnke of Project Adventure, PO Box 77, Hamilton, Massachusetts 01936 USA; *Playfair* by Matt Weinstein and Joel Goodman; *The Cooperative Sports and Games Book, The Second Cooperative Sports and Games Book* by Terry Orlick; and *World's Best Outdoor Games* by Glen Vecchione. Finally, no acknowledgment regarding outdoor activities can omit Outward Bound which originated the use of outdoor initiative games for training.

These are my primary sources and not necessarily the origins of these activities. I apologize in advance for any omissions of credit.

CMC

ix

1

Introduction

Twenty years of using experiential games and the outdoors has deepened my appreciation for their applicability and relevance in a variety of learning contexts. Whether it was fellow members of the Baha'i Faith learning the principles of consultation, a university class on creative problem solving, or a team of corporate executives planning the transformation of their organization's culture, learning was significantly enhanced through "workplay," or the use of games in the outdoors.

"Workplay" connotes the nature of not only the educational process it describes but also the creative organizational culture that it promotes. In the midst of a storm of shifting priorities, chaos, and ambiguity, organizations are becoming the students and the educators of the fundamentals of a nascent global cultural transformation. Consensus, full and frank discussion, multiple perspectives, empowerment, teamwork, consultation, and co-operation are consistently proving to be the means not only to stay afloat but also to achieve quality, continuous improvement, innovation, and high performance.

A new world order of values and perceptions is emerging. Unity is emerging in the midst of our growing awareness and experience of diversity and the paradoxes it engenders. The workplace is becoming the crucible in which new ways of leading, following, relating, and being with one another are tested and refined. Organizations are becoming to the world community what families are to the local community, paradoxically both the seeds and the harvest of fundamental values and paradigms.

Work is being infused with new expectations and a new spirit. It is being elevated to a new status, one that is more akin to joy and worship than inconvenience and drudgery. Training and trainers assume a greater status and responsibility in this light. It is my hope that the ideas and activities in this book help meet the new challenges and opportunities that are unfolding.

The Great Outdoors

Being outdoors in a setting of natural beauty provides an appropriate context for holistic learning. Outdoor games engage our physical, emotional, and spiritual bodies as well as our minds. Natural surroundings and fresh air energize. The woods and forest beckon us back to our primitive roots, to a place that Shakespeare's plays depicted as full of spirits, magic, and emotion. Blue sky, red sunsets, white puffy clouds, green fields speckled with wild flowers, pine-covered paths, moonlit meadows, crickets chirping, birds singing, snow crunching under foot, the smell of spring thaw, summer sweetness, autumn decay, a salty breeze, burning leaves, the squish of mud, the sting of hot sand, and the cold of snow are just a few among a plethora of sensory images we experience while outdoors. These sensations often tap emotionally and spiritually uplifting memories.

Outdoor games offer an opportunity to add an element of fun, exhilaration, and adventure to a training program. The outdoors recaptures the sense of wonder and playful discovery that we first gleaned while playing outside as children. These games can transform the post-lunch or mid-program feeling of inertia into a playful and effective recess that tests and reinforces learning themes that were previously presented didactically.

Play

Outdoor games are an ideal theater for experiential learning. Playing games can set the stage for the dramatic opening act of a training program. The contrast they provide in both training mode and environment enhances understanding in much the same way that Shakespeare's comic interludes highlight the themes of his famous tragedies. Certain of these outdoor games are also particularly well suited as the final act in a training program. They allow the players to exit with a moving and memorable experience.

Outdoor games change both awareness and behavior by presenting learning opportunities that challenge participants' assumptions and usual patterns of thought and behavior. By presenting immediate and compelling problems they prime participants to search beyond routine behaviors and thinking frames. Creative ways of perceiving, doing, and being can and do arise spontaneously from the fun-and-games atmosphere of these outdoor activities. When this new learning is experienced as useful and is associated with the pleasurable emotions of play, it is likely to endure.

Teamwork

Outdoor games offer a much-needed and essential means for groups to learn about and develop teamwork. While such games address issues such as communication, decision making, creativity, problem solving, and goal setting, they are particularly relevant for building the trust, mutual understanding, and appreciation of individual differences that are critical for successful teamwork. In the world of sports, music, and theater, teams, orchestras, or groups are routinely expected to practice or rehearse together to prepare themselves for peak performance. Gradually, individual ability and initiative are integrated into the unique and dynamic context of the team in a trial-and-error process of osmosis. Team effectiveness is a function of how well individual talent and ability are assimilated and utilized. Thus team performance depends primarily on the patterns of trust, timing, and interaction that have developed between and among members. These patterns develop best in the safe environment of practice and rehearsal where errors are opportunities for playful learning, not serious loss. Outdoor games provide just such a learning atmosphere.

Fantasy Scenarios

Many of the activities in this book contain scenarios that create a fantasy back-drop or rationale for a game. These can be typed, copied, and handed to participants or used as a trainer guide, depending on the nature of the activity. The scenarios contain all the information necessary for the group to understand the nature of the challenge. They include rules, constraints, and safety considerations. The games thus establish a dramatic context and a goal that, to be achieved, requires the group to work as a team. The participants are like actors in a play. They determine the outcome of the scene through the way they play their parts. You, as the trainer, attentively observe them in the role of a member of the audience.

While the games depict imaginary situations, their scripts are internally consistent and realistic in conveying how and why the group is constrained in its particular predicament. This approach facilitates and maintains the suspension of reality required to engage the participants. The deeper the level of their participation the more motivated they will become to develop the teamwork attitude and behaviors necessary to succeed in the activity. These same behaviors and attitudes will be applicable to the accomplishment of real work goals.

2

Trainer Guidelines

The outdoor games described in this book, together with the information in the **Introduction** and in these guidelines, allows both the novice and experienced trainer to easily and confidently facilitate the games. While those more experienced outdoor trainers may take liberty and even issue with some of these guidelines, the novice outdoor trainer will find them invaluable. In any case these trainer guidelines should be read and reviewed routinely until the issues, if not the specific solutions and suggestions offered, are automatically assimilated into your approach to using these outdoor activities.

Preparation

The two crucial components to introducing outdoor games are logistical preparation and psychological preparation. Logistical preparation involves setting the stage for the games in a manner that keeps participants unaware of what is to come. Some of the influence of these games lies in the drama that they evoke. Knowing what is coming reduces the surprise and novelty of the challenge.

In preparing a game, minimize surprises. The human factor supplies more than enough uncertainty in these exercises. Never allow participants to use a material setup that you have not directly experienced, tested, or observed under conditions similar to those in which it will be implemented. Pretest all the elements, boats, shuttles, bridges, etc. that participants will build and/or use during a particular exercise. Variability in kind, quality, and quantity of materials and the fit between them and group size, in terms of a group's number and physical stature, makes testing a practical necessity. Failure to test can lead to the challenge being so easy or so difficult that boredom or frustration hinders its potential as a learning experience.

Once logistical preparation is complete, begin the psychological preparation by creating a safe and engaging atmosphere. Before joining the participants, assume the persona of a storyteller/director who is about to prepare his or her cast. Convey a sense of drama about the activity. Your goal is to facilitate each game's capacity to transform the training into a fantasy adventure. The games are designed to disguise real work issues enough to allow them to be worked through or re-enacted during the game. A review or summary can then draw parallels between the activity of the game and work situations as and when participants volunteer them.

Establishing a reassuring environment that encourages playful yet serious participation must be accomplished during the introduction of a program. The critical issues that any introductory presentation should convey at the outset to ensure that the stage is properly set for structured outdoor experiences are as follows:

1. Laughter and fun are encouraged.

2. The training is experiential, that means participants will be interacting physically, emotionally, mentally, and spiritually.

3. Safe touching will be necessary in order to accomplish certain challenges.

4. The training bears no relationship to T-groups or encounter groups.

5. Participants will work as a unit or in subgroups to accomplish specific goals that will require their co-operative effort to accomplish.

6. Review or summary will follow each activity in order to discuss what happened, what worked and what didn't, how they felt about what they did, and any improvement plans to be applied to future challenges.

7. The program is not Outward Bound. Physical strength, aerobic conditioning, and athletic ability are not necessary. People of any age and level of physical fitness can participate—and have participated.

8. Interaction with those whom they don't know well is encouraged.

9. Goal accomplishment depends on transferring or making connections between what happens during the training activities and parallel work situations.

10. Experiential learning requires full participation and a playful attitude. Let the child within come out to play.

11. Challenge by choice. Refrain from "volunteering" or pressuring members of the group to participate. Freedom is essential to the achievement of an atmosphere of challenge and fun.

12. There is always a meaningful role for those who opt not to do some aspect of an activity. Sometimes these less active roles are specified; they include evaluator, judges, safety checker, and observer/reporter.

Challenge Level

Determining the degree of difficulty of an activity for a particular group is important. Difficulty has three parameters: physical, psychological, and intellectual. Physical challenge involves how much strength, agility, stamina, or physical co-ordination a challenge demands of a group. The level of perceived risk or danger of an exercise constitutes its psychological challenge. How perplexing it is to solve a challenge through the use of logic, visualization, and creativity determines intellectual difficulty.

All these areas should be considered in setting up an activity. They are often interrelated. Sometimes the number and/or size of resources suggested in the materials and procedure sections are approximations. In these activities, make judgments based on how the three parameters of difficulty will be affected. Anticipate how the addition or deletion of resources or the use of larger or smaller materials will work out. Consider a particular group's needs and ability relative to the areas of challenge, the goals of the program, and how important success or failure is at the point at which the activity is introduced. These issues relate to the art of training with outdoor games. There are no hard-and-fast rules. Given the challange of trying to prepare an activity that is neither too easy nor too demanding, the following general guidelines are useful:

1. Discuss the physical, psychological, and intellectual difficulty factors with the participants. Ask them what level of challenge they want, based on a ten-point scale. The decision can be by consensus, majority vote, or an averaging of all the votes, whichever is most suitable to the group.

   If more than one activity is being used, start with those with minimal, if any, variability in terms of materials required. Then during review or summary check with the group periodically about the degree and areas of difficulty. Ask the participants what they want and whether they are getting it. This process gives them ownership which, while it does not guarantee the ideal level of challenge, does make the occasional misjudgment much easier to manage.

2. Start with lower levels of difficulty and gradually increase the gradient.

3. Just because a task is handled competently and with minimal effort, or abandoned after a frustrating failure, that does not necessarily mean that the learning objectives of the activity have not been achieved. Use the review or summary to examine how the easy success affected morale and improved the group's teamwork. The hallmark of an effective challenge is its capacity to build team spirit by requiring full group participation to meet it successfully. The quick-and-easy solution tends to leave people out of the process and therefore deflates morale.

   Those challenges that end in defeat and frustration usually draw the most poignant lessons. Use the review or summary to emphasize what worked and underscore what was learned and how to avoid repeating mistakes. If the activity was particularly difficult due to a trainer misjudgment about what resources to supply, acknowledge that the participants had a particularly difficult task. It is all right to say that you erred by underestimating the degree of difficulty of the exercise. Always avoid any possibility of giving the group the impression that you overrated them.

4. Err on the side of greater difficulty after a group has succeeded, and on the side of lesser difficulty after they have failed.

5. Avoid back-to-back failures. Back-to-back successes are OK.

6. If you are only doing one outdoor exercise, make it one in which success is likely.

7. If you are conducting several outdoor games with the same group, plan for one or more "failures," particularly when working with an intact group and/or when team building is a learning goal. Valuable diagnostic information about (a) what a group needs to change and develop in terms of performance and (b) the group's level of commitment and trust is revealed and readily available during review or summary after a misadventure. Two or more such "failures" simply allow the comparative opportunity to gauge progress.

8. Include a contingency plan in case you discover midstream that an activity is too difficult. Be ready with options such as offering additional materials, loosening the constraints, modifying the rules, and allowing more time. Use these back-up measures judiciously and only after consulting the group about their willingness to accept them. Ideally, give participants a choice among several modifications.

9. Have a contingency plan that will make a challenge more difficult once it is underway. Do this in a manner that avoids the perception that you are "making up the rules as you go along." This perception can undermine the credibility that is central to your effectiveness. Credibility is usually threatened when your actions raise questions about your impartiality, fairness, and trustworthiness. A direct way to deal with this is simply to ask a group if they want a little more challenge. There are also certain exercises that lend themselves to foreshadowing your intervention.

   Foreshadowing involves the possibility of some handicap ensuing after the exercise gets underway. Introduce it at the start of the exercise. Stipulate that the nature of the handicap makes it unpredictable in terms of when, who, and for how long it will endure. This qualification affords the necessary latitude regarding how and even whether to implement it. Foreshadowing is useful not only in salvaging an activity that seems to lack sufficient challenge but also in allowing you to alter the dynamics of the group by handicapping certain members. Silencing a leader or paralyzing some or all of the participants are examples that frequently create new and edifying interactions.

   A standard foreshadowing would be the announcement that there is a plague in the area, which is highly contagious. The consequences of the plague can be one or more of the following handicaps: blindness, muteness, or paralysis of one or more limbs. Be sure to specify what the effects of the plague might be and indicate that you will notify participants if they are stricken and when and if they recover. Don't use foreshadowing until you are familiar with how an activity runs without it. Foreshadowing helps in adjusting degree of difficulty as well as in exploring particular aspects of group interaction. A caveat involves the danger of overtaxing the person who is handicapped. Being blind or mute can be frustrating and the combination is quite difficult to cope with. Remain sensitive to how handicapped participants are faring and be prepared to have the handicap disappear or temporarily go into remission.

10. End a program with a challenge that is likely to be met successfully.

11. If you are unfamiliar with the activity and/or unsure of the consequences, test your assumptions with a trial run before deciding whether or not to use it.

Safety

Physical and psychological safety standards are established by:
1. The introductory remarks.

2. The relative lack of danger inherent in the activities themselves.

3. The provision of explicit trainer and participant information about potential dangers.

4. Repeated trainer emphasis on safety as a program goal.

5. Written and oral instruction that it is incumbent upon the participants to ensure each other's well-being.

Make it a habit to say at the outset of each game, "As a team, your first responsibility is to each other's safety and well-being. This mission involves real hazards that must be guarded against to ensure a safe and successful outcome."

There is one specific safety rule that warrants mention and that relates to the instruction that participants are not to physically jump off any element during the program. Sprained ankles are the common consequence of jumping.

There are two other factors that affect safety and therefore require consideration: participants' physical condition and weather. Outdoor activities, even those that are not particularly strenuous, demand extra precautions. A simple and effective measure is to obtain brief medical histories that include current medications, allergies and any physical limitations, illnesses or long-standing injuries. Follow up with questions about any responses that indicate potential physical limitations. Probe participants' answers to questions about medical status. This approach assures safety and assists those with medical conditions to participate fully in an appropriate fashion.

Adverse weather can jeopardize an outdoor program because it presents both inconvenience, in terms of discomfort, and greater safety concerns. There is no simple rule or easy way to gauge when to postpone an outdoor program because of inclement weather. Foul weather can sometimes actually provide a more dramatic and challenging environment that bonds participants in their endeavor. It can also dampen spirits and create a nuisance factor that detracts from the experience. Raise the issue with the group at a preliminary meeting. Once the program is in progress, use observation of the experience, periodic group preference checks, and safety considerations to decide. Ease of rescheduling is a factor if inconvenience rather than safety is at issue. "If in doubt, try it out" is certainly consistent with an experiential approach. Use the safer exercises first when following this maxim. Ultimately there are no guarantees with regard to safety when doing outdoor activities given the many variables involved. Experience with these activities and consulting and/or training with experts in safety such as Project Adventure or Outward Bound are helpful in gaining skill and confidence. Remember that challenge by choice applies to whether, how, and with whom you use the activity as well as to whether and how participants will be involved in it.

Explanations

Some games are specifically designed to be led by the trainer, while others leave the option to either give the participants a written explanation or to use the description as a prompt for verbally directing the activity until the procedure is memorized. Giving participants a written description of outdoor games can add reality and clarity to the challenge.

Be an inconspicuous observer during the action. Answer only those questions that are of a technical nature. Handle most other questions by informing participants that they have all the information necessary to accomplish the task. If they ask questions about the rules or the task participants should generally be referred back to their instruction sheets, which contain all the information necessary to accomplish the task. Such questioning usually reflects the onset of the problem-solving process. Avoid giving the group unwarranted clues by responding.

Have a pocket-sized notebook handy to record significant events. Give participant observers specific observation guidelines and/or similar notepads.

Stop Action

There are two occasions when the trainer should intervene. The first occurs when any action appears to present a safety hazard, and the second is when the trainer calls for a stop in the action to ask the group to examine how it is proceeding because they seem to be stuck. Both these instances are judgment calls. Safety timeouts should be used whenever a safety issue arises. In marginal cases the group can be asked if they think a safety timeout should be called. The trainer always has the last word on safety. Make the "Stop action" call a little beyond the point of your discomfort with the procedure to give the group maximum opportunity to work things out for themselves.

Cameras

Use both still and video cameras whenever possible given the splendid photo opportunities these outdoor games offer. Assign a separate person to handle the photography. The trainer needs to be fully attuned to the action. Review the photos and/or video at a follow-up meeting to discuss the program and/or changes that have subsequently occurred. Such a review recaptures, in a dramatic fashion, the fun, spirit, and learning that transpired. Edit the video if possible and add music and captions to increase its impact. If time is available during the program, use video reviews in the evening to indelibly highlight portions of the action that were either particularly edifying or worthy of more indepth analysis. Many groups create photo-collages that are prominently placed in the workplace as a memento. These serve to further both the fun and the goals of the program. If necessary, obtain permission ahead of time to take photographs or videos.

Review

Review immediately after each game. This is the trainer's opportunity to guide the group toward critical reflection on what has just transpired. Concentrate on the stated goals of the program. There are, however, many related and tangential issues that may need to be addressed depending on how the activity progressed. Initially, allow the group to discuss what happened during the event. When questions arise directed at solutions to the problem and performance comparisons with other groups, remind the group that the emphasis is on the way they work together and not how to solve the challenges. Ask the group to describe what it was that they did to meet or attempt to meet the challenge. Also inquire about what feelings were elicited and the degree of participation and ownership that each experienced.

It is helpful to have participants respond privately and in writing to handouts of review questions, especially those that ask for assessment of personal feelings and participation level. Writing while outdoors, however, is sometimes cumbersome and usually requires pads or clipboards. It is worth the extra time and effort to make large, laminated index cards with prepared questions that are geared to learning objectives. The cards are repeatedly referred to during the program and can even be taken back to the workplace at its conclusion.

In general, and especially when team building is an important goal of the program, establish a review or summary procedure that concentrates on the group, group dynamics, and interactional patterns rather than on individual behavior and personalities. This approach produces a safer and more productive discussion of an activity and individual issues that need addressing are handled, however circumspectly. Nonproductive personality bashing and defensiveness are diminished, if not altogether avoided.

Team building with intact groups often reveals the existence of one or more individuals who are scapegoats for the team's inability to collaborate and/or perform effectively. Frequently scapegoats accentuate their already basically different orientation in response to covert or overt attempts to make them conform to the dominant group. Differing orientations lead to an impasse when groups are unable to see diversity as something to be welcomed and incorporated rather than ridiculed and extinguished. They lead to infighting which often divides organizations along formal or informal lines and generate endless non-productive meetings, rehashings, and grievances that poison morale and sap performance and profit. Such impasses are a common and increasingly debilitating problem given the emerging dual developments of incorporating a more diverse work force and making teamwork the norm for getting things accomplished in organizational life.

If such an individual focus on review or summarie with such groups is permitted, they invariably mirror the personality-directed accusations that occur at work. An "either/or" struggle rather than a "both/and" dynamic develops. Each side self-righteously accuses the other of one form of intolerance or another. Both sides are right about each other's intolerance and therefore both sides are wrong in terms of their approach to working together effectively.

Person-centered review sessions are especially inappropriate for intact groups for two basic reasons. First, it is easy for a trainer to fall into the trap of choosing sides because he or she is often predisposed by personality type to one or the other side of the conflict. Second, taking sides is disastrous as it intensifies the struggle by giving it legitimacy. It is an illegitimate struggle from a systems perspective in that both sides are necessarily interconnected and therefore an inclusive "both/and" rather than a divisive "either/or" solution is essential for the integrity of that system. Unfortunately, finding an internal or external enemy to scapegoat is emotionally gratifying, while looking for the problem in the system is hard work.

Taking sides may sometimes give the impression of resolving differences, but this is usually due to politeness on the part of the "conforming party." Follow-up invariably demonstrates that the peace was only a temporary truce in the interests of a harmonious training. Attempts to directly alter these entrenched patterns, which resemble those of quarrelling couples, are unlikely given the time and skill needed just to get past the initial defensiveness without being seduced by one side or the other.

Blocking these patterns with a rule that requires participants to concentrate on what the group needs to do and/or what they as individuals can do to improve performance accomplishes two worthwhile ends. First, it breaks the pattern that connects most if not all the divisive, nonproductive, un-teamlike behavior that usually characterizes personality bashing and/or hostility. Second, it provokes solutions that are automatically outside the standard "change the other person" pattern that invariably fails and is what brings groups to consultants in the first place. This guideline subtly implies that the pattern of looking for a scapegoat is part of the problem while asking the group to practice new behavior that explicitly calls for a team orientation. The focus of the analysis shifts from one of finger pointing and blaming specific individuals to one of assuming individual responsibility for the group and looking at the whole group in terms of its needs. Looking for what participants can do as a group or as individuals to improve the group is both a behavioral and an attitudinal change that is conducive to better teamwork. It is adopted without first having to reject past behavior and perspectives and without losing face. Finally, the experiential nature of these exercises means that these changes are more likely to endure because their success was demonstrated in action.

Do not skip, rush, or in any way allow insufficient time for this review, which can be short-changed in an effort to include a maximum number of games because of the excitement and drama that the games can generate. The review is a critical opportunity for the group to practice this important skill and for the trainer to assure and guide learning. Allow sufficient time for the program and always ensure that the review or summary is complete before moving on to the next activity.

Sequencing

How outdoor activities are sequenced can influence their effectiveness. Generally, safer and less strenuous activities should precede those that are riskier or more physically demanding. Risk is both a psychological and a physical factor. Building trust in the group between and among participants as well as with the trainer and the program requires the careful selection and pacing of activities.

Another sequencing consideration involves the use of indoor activities. A mixture of outdoor games with more traditional training techniques can often ensure success with the full range of learning styles and agendas that a broad-based program entails. Outdoor activities are effective when used early on to break the ice and build a spirit of trust and fun that can positively infect a training atmosphere. They are also excellent to get things moving after lunch and as a way to wrap up the day with enthusiasm. Probably their most powerful use in a mixed program is to provide a practical application of theory and discussion as well as to create vivid learning metaphors that bring otherwise dry or abstract material to life.

Finally, an effective format for presenting outdoor games is to frame them as an odyssey. This approach requires the development of an overarching storyline or premise that establishes who the participants are and their mission. Each activity then becomes a sub-plot in a larger adventure. **Toxic Sludge Mobile,** (game 53), and **Earthquake I** and **Earthquake II** (games 54 and 55), plus a number of games with science fiction scenarios, can be used to create an odyssey.

1

Gold Bricks

Summary Groups of 8–12 participants are given three gold bricks and asked to balance on them without touching the ground.

Objectives To explore problem solving, quality, creativity, risk taking, and trust building.

Materials Three common bricks painted gold for each group.

Time Limit 20–30 minutes.

Procedure 1. Tell participants that their entire group is to form a human sculpture that stands solely on a pedestal of 1–3 bricks. They must keep themselves entirely on the pedestal long enough to sing a chorus from the song of their choice.

2. Review and discuss.

Commentary Facilitators should check for safety hazards. Whether you allow shoulder carries is up to you. How strict you are with touches depends on where you are with the group. A discussion of quality and standards can sometimes prove productive with this exercise. It always offers good photo opportunities.

Variation Tell multiple groups they are all representing an art colony which will win a grant if all the groups succeed and at least one demonstrates efficiency by balancing on just two bricks. A follow-up activity is to ask two groups to balance on four to five bricks. An alternative that is consistent with the theme of paying attention to and utilizing resources is to substitute three gold bars made of blocks of wood for the bricks. This approach also makes your task lighter if you have a large group and a long way to carry the materials. Make one gold bar smaller than the other two (for example, two 8-inch and one 9-inch pieces of wood cut from 2 x 4's) to create an easier activity.

2

Moon Walk

Summary   A group of 7–12 astronauts hide under a rocky outcrop during an unexpected electrical storm, which created clusters of radioactive moon dust on everything but the craters between them and their spacecraft. Their movement is hindered by the fact that they were testing an experimental oxygen system that connects the group in a line by linking people at the ankles.

Objectives   To explore problem solving, quality, interdependence, and trust building.

Materials

1. Two 10–12 foot lengths of rope laid out, 13–16 feet apart and parallel to each other. These represent the distance from the outcrop to the spaceship.

2. Four hulahoops™ spaced 12–16 inches from each other and the ropes as depicted in Figure 1.

3. Cut cross-sectional strips 1–1 1/2 inches wide of an uninflated automobile tire inner tube. Use 11 of these giant elastic bands for an astronaut group of 12, ten for a group of 11, nine for a group of ten, etc.

Time Limit   20–30 minutes.

Procedure

1. With the group on the start side of the rope, ask participants to form a line.

2. Give all but one participant a giant elastic band.

3. Describe to the group the scenario summarized above and explain that the bands represent their oxygen support system.

4. Tell participants to link themselves together at the ankles by the bands. The oxygen system should link them in an unbroken line, so that only the first and last person has a free leg.

5. Once they are properly linked, tell participants that (a) the oxygen will be used up in 15–20 minutes and (b) if anyone steps on the radioactive dust they must return to the start in order to decontaminate the person before continuing.

6. At the end of the time limit, conduct a review and discuss the activity.

Commentary   This is a good activity to use early on to start participants talking about working closely as a team and what it takes and how it feels to be connected in such a way that one's actions affect how others perform.

Variations   1. Vary the distance and angles between hoops to change the challenge level.

2. Assign time penalties for inadvertent touches instead of requiring participants to return to the start.

Figure 1. Moon Walk.

3

Blind Faith

Summary   A trust progression using blindfolds.

Objectives   To explore communication, risk taking, and trust building.

Materials
1. A large, open, level area that has good footing and several natural or set obstacles on the periphery (see "Procedure").

2. More than enough large, clean bandannas of a variety of colors and designs for each of the participants. Fold the bandannas diagonally to facilitate their use as blindfolds.

Time Limit   25–75 minutes, depending on how much you want to discuss.

Procedure
1. Explain to the group that they will be going through a progression of activities called "Blind Faith," which are designed to help them experience and examine the concepts of trust, communication, and their relationship.

2. Pass around the bandannas and ask everyone to take one.

3. Explain that the blindfolds are optional accessories and note the following: no one will be made fun of or in any way deliberately tricked or embarrassed while blindfolded. The blind will be protected. A "Freeze!" command will be used if there is a need to stop the action for safety reasons. Peeking is a matter of challenge by choice. If anyone does peek, they should do so in an inconspicuous manner that will not make the accomplishment of the team's task easier. They are on the honor system.

4. Ask the group to put on their blindfolds. Once they are "blind," explain that their first task is to line up according to height, from tallest to shortest, without speaking. Tell the group they should raise their hands when they think they have completed their task. When the group is ready, ask them to take off their blindfolds and discuss how they communicated and what it felt like doing the activity.

5. When the review is complete, ask the participants to fold their hands and note whether their right or left thumb is on top. Ask them to pair up with someone with a different thumb dominance (that is, rights with lefts). If the

group has more of one thumb dominance than another, allow those with the same thumb dominance to pair up.

6. Tell the group that the next activity will involve being either blind or mute and that each will get a chance to experience both. Ask them to decide who will be blind first.

7. Once the blindfolds are on, remind the mutes that they can make no sound whatever and that they should be careful with the precious bodies in their trust.

8. Explain that the mutes are to lead the blind safely around the area until you signal them to switch roles.

9. Give each pair 3–4 minutes before consulting about the experience.

10. Ask participants to hop on one foot and pair up with someone who is hopping on the opposite foot from theirs.

11. Explain that this activity will duplicate the previous blind-mute experience, only the blind person is also mute. Allow participants a turn each of 2–3 minutes.

12. Tell the group that the last challenge has two parts. In the first part, their only means of contact will be by holding opposite ends of the mute person's bandanna. The second phase will be the same as the first except the blind person is also mute and at a point somewhere near an obstacle (for example, a wall, boulder, fence, chair, table). The mute person will leave the blind person and regain speech in order to talk the blind and mute person over, under, around, onto, or through the obstacle. Since they will not be able to touch each other, emphasize that they must be extra careful.

13. Let the first phase go for 2–3 minutes, then signal the pairs to begin the second phase. Remind them of its constraints. After they have all negotiated the obstacles, tell them to switch roles and repeat the sequence.

14. Don't rush the review session.

Commentary

This activity is rich in both the cognitive and emotional material that it brings up for people. Differences in giving and receiving feedback, support, challenges, and expectations raise many issues related to styles and perceptions about what is enough when it comes to communication, trust, and risk taking. The activity is best used early on in a team-building program. **Blind and Mute Carry** (game 50) is a good companion activity, but it should not be used too soon after this one.

Variation

The sequence is one of graduated steps and therefore it is best to keep to the order in case you want to skip some of the activities. The sequence can be separated by lunch or another activity. A mid-level challenge is for participants to line up by birthday, month and day, being both blind and mute. This same challenge is a good ice-breaker for a group that is only mute.

4

The Ladder of Success

Summary
A group of seven or more participants create a ladder using wooden dowels that each can climb across.

Objectives
This exercise simulates climbing the ladder of success. It can be used as a metaphor to discuss how individuals succeed in organizations and/or dichotomous issues such as risk/trust, individual initiative/group support, and independence/interdependence in teamwork.

Materials
Three or more hardwood dowels 1 inch or more in diameter and 3 feet long.

Time Limit
15 minutes.

Procedure

1. Ask for a volunteer to be the first climber. With even-numbered groups there will be a second climber.

2. Tell the remainder of the group to pair up, based on similarity of height, and give each twosome a dowel.

3. Explain that the dowels are rungs of the ladder. Have each pair facing with the rung between them. Ask them to hold the ends of each rung with two hands and to form a horizontal ladder by standing shoulder to shoulder with the other pairs.

4. Tell participants to determine the shape of the ladder by adjusting each step between crotch and shoulder height.

5. Explain that once the climber safely passes a rung the pair holding it moves to the end of the ladder so as to extend it. Note that each climber succeeds by crossing the length of the ladder twice.

6. Note that once the initial climber(s) succeeds, he or she takes the last rung and the person(s) holding it has the option of climbing. Make it clear that climbing the ladder of success is optional and that those who initially choose not to will have another opportunity at the end.

7. Begin the exercise once you are satisfied that all the participants understand the task and the need for everyone to make sure that the process stops if someone is tiring or struggling to hold up their end.

8. Watch the proceedings closely and be ready to step in with assistance if needed.

9. Conduct a review and discussion.

Commentary

This exercise provides rich discussion as it touches on the themes of trust and the individual versus the team. These are matters that must be openly discussed and experienced before a group can truly function as a team.

Walking the ladder is relatively simple as participants can steady themselves by crouching and touching heads and shoulders. The difficult part is supporting heavier participants, especially when they pause on one step.

From a safety perspective you should use only smooth sturdy dowels and examine them before use. Make sure to have thicker dowels on hand in case there are very heavy participants.

Variations

1. The basic ways to enrich this exercise involve varying the ladder. It can be lengthened to three extensions or success can be a specific boundary. The ladder can be modified to contain turns and obstacles that must be negotiated along the way.

2. An interesting option is to allow the climber to predetermine what success will be based on the length and shape of the ladder, i.e., set his or her own challenge level. The team can also define what constitutes success, both self- and other-determined success such as "personal best" or some other criteria, if time allows.

5

A Weighty Problem

Summary
Two teams of 4–10 members are opposite each other. Each complete team needs to reach the opposite side in the fewest possible carries.

Objectives
To explore creative problem solving, co-operation versus competition, and trust building.

Materials
1. Two tables or sturdy platforms. Each must be able to hold one team without tipping during the activity. Well-built picnic or wooden tables and even large flat boulders will suffice. If you are unsure of the table strength, leave it out (see "Variations").

2. A bandanna for each participant to use as a blindfold.

Time Limit
30 minutes.

Procedure
1. Place the tables opposite each other. Make the distance between the two consistent with the strength and athleticism of the group, using 25–50 feet as a range.

2. Divide the group into two teams. Direct each team to one of the tables and explain that the table nearest them is their starting line and the one farthest from them is their safety zone.

2. Give the group enough bandannas for each member and a prepared information sheet (Handout 5.1), and concentrate your attention on being ready to prevent any mishaps in carrying or unloading.

3. Conduct a review and discussion.

Commentary
Always attend to safety and be ready to assist when the last person is brought up onto the safety platform.
Creativity issues are related to imposing rules where there are none. For example, some groups assume only one person can carry another person. Another example that relates to co-operation versus competition is the often-ignored fact that if members of one team carry those of the opposite team, it doesn't count as a carry. Even when groups discover this means of minimizing their carries, competitiveness can complicate matters. Will one team carry the other's

last member? If they do, their last member has to roll across the ground and be credited with one more carry than the opposition.

Variations

1. Greater distances, such as 60–100 feet, can be used if you omit the "no hands or feet" rule and allow the last person to hop across on one foot instead. As noted above, omit the tables whenever there is any doubt about their strength.

2. This activity can also work well with just one team or when the goal is speed rather than the least number of carries.

Information Sheet

Your task is to get your entire team from the starting line to the designated safety zone using a minimum number of carries and without violating any of the following constraints:

- The only way for you to get from here to there is to be carried while blind. If you must peek, do so inconspicuously.

- Anyone touching the ground while in transit must return to the starting line.

- Once you are in the safety zone, you must remain there.

- A carry occurs each time you transport a teammate to the safety zone.

You may be wondering how the last member of your team can reach the safety zone without being carried. He or she can go from the starting line to the safety zone as long as no hands or feet touch the ground or are otherwise used for propulsion. Such a crossing counts toward your total score as one carry.

You have all the information you need to solve the problem.

Remember to handle your precious cargo safely and gently. Use extra caution when loading and unloading.

6

Toss

Summary   Two teams compete with at least one umpire, in a relay race that involves tossing water balloons.

Objectives   To explore teamwork, creativity, competition, planning, and ethics.

Materials   1. Water balloons.

2. Powdered lime, chalk, or rope to make the boundary lines.

Time Limit   25–45 minutes depending on the size of the teams.

Procedure

1. Prepare the site of the activity as follows:

   a. Fill half as many balloons as there will be participants in each of the two relay teams. Over-inflate one balloon and under-inflate another to see if the participants examine their resources. Each team must have an even number of members as they will cross the field in pairs. Put each team's water balloons in separate bags.

   b. Mark off a rectangular field that is 30–40 feet wide by 60–100 feet long. The smaller boundaries represent the starting line and the turn-around point.

   c. Place the two teams' balloon bags at opposite corners of the starting line.

2. Once preparation is complete, bring the group to the site and do the following:

   a. Appoint at least one volunteer to be the umpire/observer. Then divide the remainder of the group into two even-numbered teams of identical size (for example 6–6, 8–8, 10–10, 12–12). Groups of four are too small. Larger groups are best formed into four teams with the winners of the initial matches playing each other, unless you are using this exercise primarily as an energizer.

   b. Explain that this activity is a relay race. Teams form pairs to take turns tossing water balloons to each other until one of them catches it at the opposite boundary. Then the water balloon is again tossed back until it is passed to one of the members of the next pair behind the starting line. This process continues until one of the last pair has returned the object to her/his partner behind the starting line. The winner of the relay is the first to finish.

    c.   Assign each team to one corner or the other and tell them their balloons are in the bag. Then give each team and each umpire a copy of the rules on Handout 6.1. Tell the teams that they have 10–15 minutes to form pairs and decide on a strategy.

    d.   Tell the umpire(s) that they are the final arbiters and must strictly enforce the rules. Point out to them that the main thing to watch for is taking too many steps and not picking up all the bits of burst balloon. Note that the umpire should not rule on blocking or other obstructions that may go on between opposing teams.

3. At the end of the time limit, answer any questions and then ask the umpire to signal the start.

4. Conduct a review and discussion.

Commentary

This is an energizing activity that raises many issues about how groups work together. Those who are less physically inclined, or handicapped, can participate as umpires. If you have an umpire team, ask them to observe at the planning session and to comment on the game during the review. Sometimes teams handicapped by someone with "hands like feet" use hats or other clothing to create a softer and larger catching target. Discuss these catching options during the review or summary, especially if creativity is a focal point.

Variations

1. Shorten the field and eliminate steps for a less physically demanding game.

2. Vary the number of steps from none to four. A narrower field increases the incidence of competitive interaction between teams.

3. The substitution of large-diameter balls, rubber chickens, frisbees, and other odd throw toys adds to the fun and creativity.

4. As well as water balloons, use raw eggs and other hard-to-throw objects. Since all the objects must be used, the challenge entails considerable negotiation as each pair makes its choice.

Rules

1. The balloon must always be tossed. It may never be rolled, handed off, or anything else that is not a pass through the air.
2. You may not take more than two steps while holding the balloon. If you do, your pair must start again.
3. If you drop the balloon, your pair must pick it up and begin all over again.
4. If you intercept the other team, you can throw or roll the balloon as far away as you wish and they must retrieve it and start again.
5. If you drop the balloon while trying to intercept it, you must start again and the other team automatically skips to its next pair.
6. If you burst a balloon, pick up all the pieces before starting again.
7. If you burst the other team's balloon while trying to intercept, you must give the other team a balloon.
8. If a team bursts all its balloons, they automatically lose.
9. Be careful of one another's safety!

7

Spilt Milk

Summary
A group is presented with a nearly full can of milk, which is in the middle of a circular boundary. The milk is radioactive and has contaminated everything within the circle. The group has a bag of materials to use in getting the milk safely into a protective container for proper disposal.

Objectives
To explore creative group problem solving.

Materials

1. A bag containing a ball of twine, two pairs of scissors, a quarter section of automobile tire inner tube, a large container with a screw top, a large pair of preferably old, stiff fireplace gloves, a large tin canister with one end open, and anything else you may want to add. The screw-top container should be larger than the tin canister. The size of the canister should be such that if a strip of the inner tube 1–1 1/2 inches wide were cut into a large elastic band it would fit snugly around the canister. One solution is to tie strings to a couple of such elastic bands and have several people stretch them over the canister. The canister can then be carried off.

2. A duplicate of the open canister described above filled to within 1 1/2 –2 inches of the top with milk that is colored with red food dye.

3. A rope 80 feet or more long or enough powdered lime to create a circle 20–25 feet in diameter.

Time Limit
45–75 minutes.

Procedure
In advance of the activity:

1. Locate a private open space of ground and form a circle 20–25 feet in diameter using rope or powdered lime. Rope is simpler but lime will mark shoes, making a perimeter touch easy to confirm.

2. Place the canister of milk in the center of the circle.

3. Once the stage is set take the group to the site, briefly explain the task and ask for volunteers to observe and referee whether or not someone has become contaminated. Two or three observers and five to nine participants works best.

4. Give the participants the bag and tell them the following:

"The encircled can contains radioactive milk. The cordoned-off area represents the area that has been contaminated given the radius in that the milk's radioactivity can be harmful. Anyone coming any closer than that radius will be contaminated and suffer anything from loss of speech to death. The observers will call any contaminations. Participants may not make deliberate sacrifices in their effort to dispose of the milk. Time is of the essence. In 30–45 minutes an oxygen transformation reaction will occur and the milk's contamination radius will increase exponentially, threatening all life in its path.

"The bag contains a special container. Once the milk is in this container it can be safely approached and sealed off by putting on the lid. Safety gloves have been provided for this purpose. Participants may use only the materials provided to retrieve the milk. These materials represent the kit that has been specially designed to safely deactivate radioactive substances. Unfortunately the technicians whom you supervise and who do the deactivation have gone on strike, and thus the job is yours."

5. Announce that the activity has begun and remind participants of the time limit and the consequences of getting too close to the milk or failing in their task.

6. Early on, notify one of the observers that loss of speech will occur if someone violates the perimeter of the circle or gets closer than a 10–12 foot radius to the can prior to its being put inside the protective container.

7. Conduct a review after the task has been accomplished or when time runs out.

Commentary

This game is not very active and is suitable as an indoor exercise. Smaller groups of 5–6 are preferable given the nature of the task. Spills are not uncommon and you can get into an interesting discussion of standards by asking participants to rate how safely the exercise was performed based on spilling and individual contamination. Ask participants to write privately a number from 1–10, with ten being totally safe, and to discuss their ratings, first in groups of two or three and then in the full group.

Variations

1. Cutting the inner-tube strips ahead of time is recommended for this activity which has been used under the name of **Toxic Waste** and **Hot Stuff**, among others, in its long use. The strips facilitate the process while reducing creativity.

2. A plastic bag makes for some creative solutions and illustrates the transformation of a "container" into a "tool."

8

Eight-pointed Star

Summary   One or two groups of eight stand in a circle and toss a water balloon between them in the pattern of an eight-pointed star. Once this seemingly simple task is accomplished participants are presented with a more challenging problem related to the star pattern they have learned. Observers are used.

Objectives   To explore communciation, leadership, and problem solving.

Materials   A bag of five moderately filled water balloons for each group of eight. (Only one balloon per group is needed but accidents do happen!)

Time Limit   30–45 minutes.

Procedure

1. Briefly describe the activity and ask participants to form one or two groups of eight with one or more volunteer observers for each group.

2. Place a balloon in the middle of each group and instruct participants as follows:

   "Stand in a circle. Your initial task is to toss the water balloon between yourselves in the pattern of an eight-pointed star. The pattern must be continuous and involve all eight of you as points of the star. You may begin."

3. Give each observer an instruction sheet, Handout 8.1.

4. When a group believes they have formed the pattern, tell them that each person should throw the balloon to someone and receive it from another. These are the only two people in the circle whom the pattern should connect. If not, they have not formed the star correctly and must reassess.

5. If the group has succeeded in forming the star, tell them their next task involves tossing the balloon to either the same person they threw it to or to the person they received it from in forming the eight-pointed star. They should begin by throwing the balloon to one of these two people. That person is out and must give the balloon to someone else who is not yet out. This person throws someone else out. When there is no one left to receive a throw, the process ends. The goal is to throw out as many people as they can, and they should keep trying to improve.

Challenge the group at some point with the fact that all eight can be eliminated.

6. Conduct a review and discussion.

Commentary   If you are using two groups, rely on the observers to let you know when a group has finished the first task. More than two groups requires an assistant or putting the observers in charge by giving them the instructions so you can roam from group to group.

Some groups have difficulty even with the first task and this is a pretty good indication of poor communication patterns and/or unproductive leadership struggles. If you sense these may be issues, use this exercise early on as a diagnostic and potential reference point for further training.

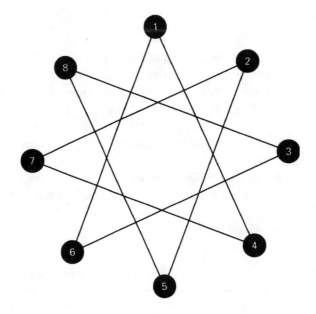

Figure 2. Eight-pointed Star.

The solution involves a pattern of one person handing the balloon to the one who is two away from them in a clockwise direction. If the points of the star are numbered from 1 to 8 (see Figure 2) the solution will be as follows: 1 to 4, 6 to 1, 3 to 6, 8 to 3, 5 to 8, 2 to 5, 7 to 2, 4 to 7. Note also the pattern of always eliminating the last person to throw. During the review, ask what patterns were noticed. There are many pattern metaphors in this exercise that you can relate to any training theme you want.

Variations   1. Balls and other objects can be substituted.

2. Catches can be restricted to one hand and penalties can be assessed for each dropped and/or burst balloon.

3. With two or more groups it can become a competition in that time penalties are assessed for drops and/or bursts.

32

Instructions for the Observer

Note the leadership and communication patterns and anything that strikes you about the way participants solve the problem. Specifics to watch for are (1) visible communication aids such as drawing a star or forming a system (such as raising hands and then lowering them) to communicate who has or has not received the balloon; and (2) insights such as observations that the balloon cannot be thrown to an adjacent person and the person who starts must also be the one who completes the star.

9

Space Escape

Summary   The team must rearrange hula hoops™, while remaining inside them, in order to create the pattern that will allow them to beam aboard their spacecraft.

Objectives   To explore team building and problem solving.

Materials   1. Six standard-size hula hoops™. The hula hoops must be easily distinguished from each other. Buy them in different colors and/or designs or tie a different color of surveyor tape on each to make them distinguishable.

   2. Nine index cards.

Time Limit   30–45 minutes.

Procedure   1. Prepare the nine index cards by putting one of the following constraints on each card:

   a.   The hoops must be arranged in a circle in order to beam up to your spacecraft.

   b.   Only one hoop may be moved at a time.

   c.   Each person must keep at least one hand on the hoop at all times.

   d.   Everyone must remain inside the hoops at all times.

   e.   Once a hoop is moved, it must be replaced in such a way that it makes contact with two other hoops.

   f.   Each hoop must always be placed so that it remains in contact with at least one of the hoops that it abutted in the original triangular pattern.

   g.   You may not adjust one hoop by moving it a little in order to allow another to squeeze in or out.

   h.   The correct solution that will allow you to beam to safety involves a sequence of four (4) moves.

   i.   The hoops must remain at approximately waist height at all times.

2. Make for each observer an observer/judge task sheet containing a copy of the nine constraints listed above, a solution (see Figure 3), and the instructions given on Handout 9.1.

3. Select a private open area free from obstructions and place the six hoops on the ground in a triangular formation (see Figure 3).

4. Briefly describe the activity and ask for two or more observer/judge volunteers.

5. Give the group the following scenario:

"You are a group of space treasure-hunters. The leaders and scientists in your expedition are trapped in an underground grotto and you must get back to your spacecraft before your oxygen runs out. The triangular pattern of hoops on the ground represents the beaming device for getting you back to safety. The device does not work in this pattern and while you all were trained in how to activate it, that was long ago and you never had any refresher courses. Some of you will be given a card describing a part of the procedure you remember. If you receive a card you may relay its information verbally to others but you may not show it to anyone. As a group you will have enough information to transform the device and beam aboard your ship. Remember that your lives and those of the remainder of your party in the cave are hanging in the balance."

6. Give the observers their task sheets and ask 1–3 participants (four is possible depending on size) to enter each hoop so that the group is relatively evenly distributed throughout the six hoops and the hoops remain in their original configuration.

7. Take questions and then distribute the nine cards so that at least one person in each hoop has one. Tell them that in 20–35 minutes their oxygen will be depleted.

8. Watch to ensure safety as they move.

9. Conduct a review when they have solved the problem or time is up.

Commentary

This activity provides both close physical contact and a challenging task that is made quite difficult given the proximity of team members. The activity requires a high level of organization and communication, especially if the group is of ten or more. It is best used by a team that has already developed some productive problem-solving methods.

Variation

A variation that allows you to alter the leadership pattern of the group involves advising participants at the outset that the oxygen levels are variable in individual tanks. Thus you can tell people who have been dominant that their warning system has indicated they must remain silent in order to preserve what little oxygen they have left.

Observer/Judge Task Sheet

Your task is to note how the group functions as a team in problem solving and to make sure they conform to the nine rules listed below. If you observe a violation of the rules, ask if anyone saw a violation before pointing it out. Confer with fellow observers or the facilitator if you are unsure about anything. As an observer of group process note how information is organized and shared. Is full and frank discussion and participation occurring? Does the group use coins or some other means to simulate their task? Be prepared to describe how the team related to each other and the task without singling out individuals in a negative fashion.

Rules

1. The hoops must be arranged in a circle in order to beam up to your spacecraft.

2. Only one hoop may be moved at a time.

3. Each person must keep at least one hand on the hoop at all times.

4. Everyone must remain inside the hoops at all times.

5. Once a hoop is moved, it must be replaced in such a way that it makes contact with two other hoops.

6. Each hoop must always be placed so that it remains in contact with at least one of the hoops that it abutted in the original triangular pattern.

7. You may not adjust one hoop by moving it a little in order to allow another to squeeze in or out.

8. The correct solution that will allow you to beam to safety involves a sequence of four (4) moves.

9. The hoops must remain at approximately waist height at all times.

Reproduced from *CHANGING PACE Outdoor Games for Experiential Learning* by Carmine M. Consalvo, HRD Press, 1996

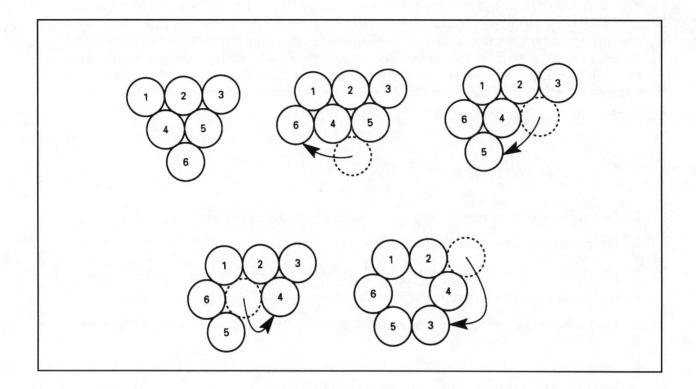

Figure 3. Space Escape: Setup and Solution.

10

The Invisible Maze

Summary

A group of astronauts in training for a 2-year mission on a space station must demonstrate their ability to learn and problem solve as a team by traversing an invisible maze.

Objectives

To explore teamwork, group problem solving, communication, leadership, and team/organizational learning.

Materials

1. A 10 x 10 foot tarpaulin, carpet, or other piece of heavy material that will not slip when walked on.

2. Graph paper.

3. Heavyweight paper or plastic folder.

Time Limit

45–75 minutes, depending on the size of the group.

Procedure

1. Draw, tape, or otherwise designate on the tarpaulin a grid eight squares across and eight squares deep. Temporary grids can be drawn in sand or marked out with powdered lime or chalk. You will also need to create four each of the grids shown in Figures 4–7. Block them out on standard-size graph paper so they will be easy to read. Then affix the graph paper inside a folder with a laminated non-see-through cover or in some other way provide a sturdy, opaque backing that will prevent participants seeing the solution through it.

2. Lay the maze out on a flat, private area near but out of sight of where you will explain the activity.

3. Tell the group they are a team of astronauts in training for an elite, high-priority NASA mission. If they qualify they will be working and living together for two years on a space station. Their challenge involves traversing an invisible maze. It is designed to allow them to demonstrate their ability to learn and problem solve as a team.

4. Note that there will also be four observer/judges representing NASA. They will beep whenever a misstep is made and monitor for examples of effective problem solving, communication, team learning, or any other designated objectives. Then ask for four volunteers to be NASA observer/

judges. More or fewer can be used depending on the group size. If you use one or two observers they may be slow with the beep responses, which can intrude on the flow of the activity. If you have more than four, have extra maze solutions available.

5. Take the NASA observer/judges over to the invisible maze. Position them at the finishing line. Then give them each a pencil, paper, a copy of the invisible maze solution, and a set of the instructions given in Handout 10.1. Tell them to read the instructions and that they can ask questions when you return.

6. Return to the astronauts and give them their task sheet, Handout 10.2.

7. Note the time and announce that the activity is officially under way as soon as you sense that the task sheet has been read. Check with the NASA group about any questions.

8. Take the group to the maze when they have finished planning.

9. Give the observers new mazes when the 30-minute time limit elapses. When the group solves the maze or the second 30 minutes is up, ask the observers to add up the number of missteps and add this total to the total elapsed time. Have a reserve set of grids at the ready in the unlikely event that participants take more than 30 minutes on the first one.

10. Conduct a review.

Commentary

This activity is ideal for 8–10 participants but can be run with fewer and even as many as 20 if organizational learning is your objective. This is a particularly effective exercise for looking at team/organizational development and learning. The task has time and performance criteria and is rich in metaphorical connections such as the roles of trial and error and deadends, investigating the unknown, transferring a vision throughout a system, going back in order to go forward, risk, ambiguity, and uncertainty.

Do not tell participants that they may move forward, sideways, diagonally, and backward. These are the legal moves, but telling them does their thinking for them and provides a valuable clue about the oft-forgotten backward move that is crucial to a solution. The issue of moving backward or backing off (for example, three steps forward, two steps back) in order to progress is an engaging metaphor to entertain during the review.

A few of the rewarding learning contexts that the maze affords are the role and development of communication systems; the response to missteps that had been made; and whether the initiative was taken, and by whom, to change the often rigid and bureaucratic system that was developed at the initial planning session.

Even the observers have to work as a team. Note whether they work collaboratively or alone in signalling and counting missteps. The fastest and most accurate systems involve redundancy or shared responsibility for these tasks versus one or two doing everything or dividing up the tasks between all four.

Variations

1. Vary the size of the grid (for example, to eight squares by nine).

2. Make missteps cost double the time if stepped on more than once.

3. Limit the planning time to 15 minutes, which can be used in the following

manner at any time: one 15-minute, three 5-minute, or one 10- and one 5-minute sessions. With this approach planning can be used more realistically. However, make it clear that, except for time used prior to the start, the planning must take place away from the maze and only involve strategy that doesn't try to verify what is already known about which spaces are and are not passable on the maze.

MAZE 1
START

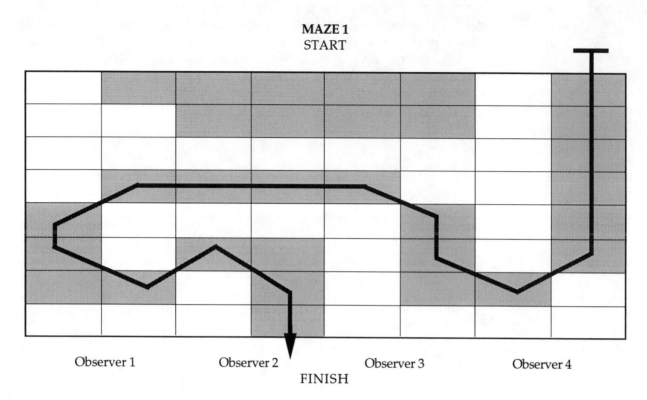

Observer 1 Observer 2 Observer 3 Observer 4

FINISH

Figure 4. Maze 1.

MAZE 2
START

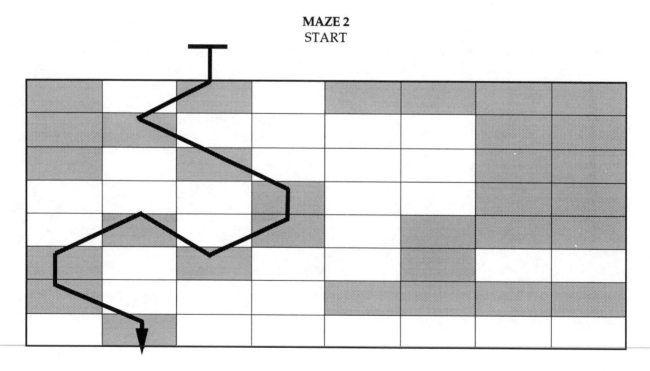

Observer 1 Observer 2 Observer 3 Observer 4

FINISH

Figure 5. Maze 2.

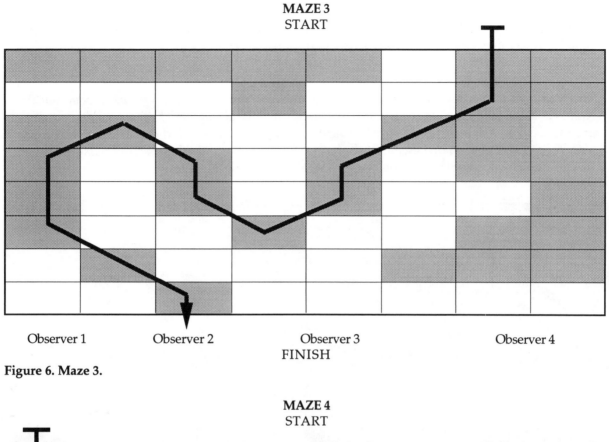

Figure 6. Maze 3.

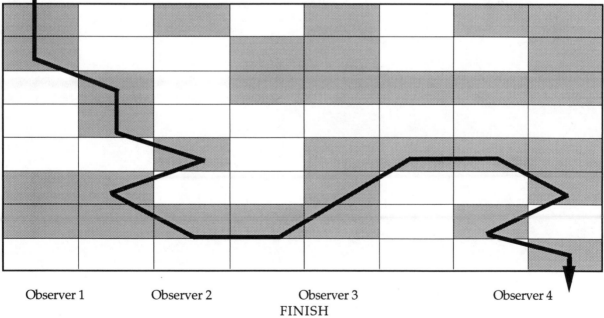

Figure 7. Maze 4.

Instructions for Observer/Judge Team

Your team's task will be to note examples of *[fill in whatever general and/or specific objectives you want]* and to raise them during the review that follows.

The astronauts will proceed through the maze one at a time. Your task will be to beep within four seconds of the time when an astronaut steps on a blank square. These unshaded squares are impassable. Give a thumbs up to indicate the square was shaded or passable. You must also keep count of each instance that someone steps on one of the blank squares. Remember that as NASA representatives you want to avoid giving hints as to which square is or isn't passable.

Reproduced from *CHANGING PACE Outdoor Games for Experiential Learning* by Carmine M. Consalvo, HRD Press, 1996

Instructions for the Astronaut Team

Goal   To get your entire group through the maze as quickly, in terms of total time (time elapsed plus one minute penalties), and as effectively, in terms of teamwork, as possible.

Constraints

1. There is at least one continuous route through the maze.

2. Arrange yourselves in an order and maintain it throughout the exercise.

3. Proceed one person at a time through the maze.

4. A legal move involves stepping one space in any direction from one square to an adjacent one with which it shares a side or corner. Pause briefly on each square as this is an old labor-intensive maze that predates the lightning-fast responses of modern-day technology.

5. Stepping on a square that is not passable results in a beep indicating that that person must leave the maze and the next person must begin again at the starting line. A thumbs-up sign indicates that the square is passable.

6. This orderly process continues until everyone is through the maze.

7. There will be a one-minute penalty assessed at the end of the activity for each misstep.

8. The maze changes every 30 minutes! The 30 minutes begin shortly. You may plan a strategy for as long as you like. Once you signal that you are ready, you will be taken to the maze. Once there you may no longer speak.

9. You have all the information you need to accomplish your mission. Do not ask the NASA observers or the facilitator for clarification. Trial and error will answer any questions you may have.

11

The Call of the Wild

Summary

An energizer for a large group (14–100 or more participants) that stimulates participants to think about training content in a playful and creative fashion.

Objectives

To use as a catalyst for opening up discussion on almost any subject or as a metaphor for aspects of creativity, leadership, and communication.

Materials

1. A large, flat, open area without any obstructions (such as trees, poles, etc.).

2. Flipchart and marker.

3. Blindfolds (optional and impractical with very large groups).

Time Limit

20–45 minutes, depending on the size of the group.

Procedure

1. Select four or more wild animals, with distinctive calls, that you think might reflect attributes related to your training theme (for example, lions for leadership or monkeys for communication). It isn't critical that each animal has a clear connection in your mind as it will be the group's task to make connections. The creativity required in drawing analogies between animals and the subject matter is often instructional for the facilitator as well as the participants. Depending on your objective and group size you may want to use some of the following: wolf, lion, owl, gorilla, elephant, snake, crow, duck, dove, mouse, and monkey.

2. Have the group form a circle leaving plenty of space between each participant. Tell the group the next exercise is "The Call of the Wild." You may want to note that wild animals have always been used as metaphors for human attributes and qualities and even in today's high-tech society sports teams are wolverines and lions rather than computers and fax machines. Then begin by asking if anyone can imitate the call of a lion, for example. Once you have had one or two responses, ask about the call of another animal, and so on for all the animals you have selected.

3. Next, ask each person to think of each of the animal calls and to select one based on the positive or negative connection that it has with the training theme (for example, leadership or co-operation). Tell the group that on your signal everyone is to close their eyes and begin doing their best

interpretation of the animal they have selected. Ask them to walk slowly, with hands out in front, without peeking. Tell them if they must take a quick look in order to feel safe they must do so discreetly and in such a way that it doesn't aid in their goal which is to group together with all their own kind —wolves with wolves, owls with owls, etc. Tell participants to open their eyes when they are sure none of their own has gone astray.

4. Take questions and then give the signal. A portable tape recorder is handy now for playing back later.

5. When all the animals have found each other, ask the participants to discuss how they felt during the experience and to come up with at least three examples each of both positive and negative attributes their animal displays that are related to the training theme. Give them 5–10 minutes before they select a reporter to share these examples with the full group.

6. Review by first asking individuals to share how they felt doing the exercise. Follow with reports of positive and negative attributes and write these on a flipchart (positives on one side and negatives on the other). Then ask how their discussion or what they heard reported has influenced their view of the training theme.

7. A good way to end is to summarize the feelings and the flipchart observations by tying those that are relevant into your own prepared mini lecture.

Commentary   This activity is an effective program starter or after-lunch energizer. Even if you are not using blindfolds, review the procedure section of **Blind Faith** (game 3) for a more extensive description of how to conduct a "blind" activity.

Variations
1. Write the names of the animals on an index card, making sure there is an even distribution of each animal. Fold the cards and randomly distribute them among the group. This approach works well with smaller groups of 10–20.

2. With groups of up to 30, divide participants evenly and then separate them by 80–100 feet. Have two cards for each animal and distribute the cards so that each person's mate is on the opposite side. This approach usually requires the inclusion of barnyard animals such as pigs, chickens, roosters, horses, donkeys, dogs, cats, cows, sheep, goats, geese, and so on.

12

Giant Space-bugs

Summary   An activity that challenges a group to free itself from a prison through logic, planning, and the effective use of their human resources.

Objectives   To explore team building, logical and creative problem solving, and leadership.

Materials   1. A flat, level, open area between two trees or posts that are 6–10 ft apart. There should be no rocks, roots, brush, or other obstructions that might cause a participant to stumble or incur injury.

2. A rope long enough to be tied between the trees.

3. 13 3 in. x 5 in. index cards.

Time Limit   45–75 minutes.

Procedure   1. Find a suitable site and tie the rope tautly between the trees. The distance between the rope and the ground should be consistent all the way across and measure about 30 inches. The height at which the rope is tied should be such that only the tallest person in the group would be able to step over it without touching.

2. Put the following 13 items of information on separate index cards so that each card contains one piece of information:

    a.   Contact with the force field anywhere from the top down activates the robots.

    b.   If the robots are activated you must all return behind the force field.

    c.   It is useless to try to overpower the robots. They are indestructible.

    d.   Contact with any part of the structure that borders the force field activates the robots.

    e.   The robots activate if they detect any vibration greater than an ordinary footfall.

    f.   The robots used to activate as soon as someone was detected beyond the force field; however, in an escape attempt yesterday, it was not until two of you were over that they activated.

g.   The robots were programmed to keep you imprisoned by giant multi-legged space bugs that look like centipedes with arms and hands that are humanoid.

h.   The space bugs are about 6 1/2 feet tall with multiple

segments about the size of a person. The more segments, the older the creature.

i.   You have a limited grasp of the space-bugs' language. You heard the boss bug say something about having to reprogram the robots because they were occasionally malfunctioning after a recent electrical storm.

j.   Do not confer until someone asks who else understands the space-bugs or the facilitator announces how much time is left. You grasp a little of the space-bugs' language. You overheard the boss bug tell her underling to deactivate the robots prior to repair by pointing at them and speaking the secret code that was a four-letter word. The boss was angry when the underling said he forgot the code because it was easy.

k.   The robots understand you through their universal language decoders but they cannot speak.

l.   The robots' sensors detect your presence as separate heat-emitting bodies.

m.   The giant bugs are warm-blooded creatures.

3. Bring the group to the site and briefly outline the activity. Then ask for between two and five volunteers to be robot guards. You need five to thirteen prisoners with nine being ideal.

4. Give the robots an instruction sheet, Handout 12.1, and tell them to review it.

5. Make sure that the index cards with the (i) and (j) information are the top two on the deck as they must be given to different people. Note that the information on the cards they are about to receive represents their personal knowledge. Emphasize that it can be shared only verbally with the others.

6. Tell the group they are adventurers who were taken prisoner by giant space-bugs. Then hand the deck to the prisoners with the information side down. Instruct them to take the top card and pass the deck along so that all the cards are distributed among all the prisoners.

7. Tell the group they have between 30 and 60 minutes before the giant space-bugs show up. Considering the rich and sumptuous food they have been fed and the way the giant space-bugs ogle them, the group may well find themselves on the menu at their next meal.

8. Once at least 10 minutes have elapsed, announce how much time is left if and when you want to activate the clue regarding the code word.

9. When they have escaped, or the time runs out, conduct a review.

Commentary This is a particularly good challenge for a team that has already demonstrated some basic trust and problem-solving ability.

Variations
1. To use more prisoners, make up additional cards so that everyone has at least one piece of information. These cards can add constraints, such as "Touching the force field will result in temporary (that is, 5 minutes) loss of speech," or "Touching the trees will result in temporary loss of sight" or simply clarifying information such as "Given the intermittent malfunctioning of the robots, you are dealing with an ambiguous environment."

2. A quicker way to run the activity is to give the prisoners all the information on one sheet rather than giving each individual a separate card or two with just one piece of information on each card.

Instructions for Robot Guards

In addition to noting how the team of prisoners performs, you are a team of robots who are guarding the alien archaeologists who are behind the force field. You have been programmed to activate and ensure that your prisoners are all behind the force field whenever any one of the following occurs:

- There is a thump as a result of a prisoner doing something like jumping, falling, or stumbling.

- More than one body is beyond the force field. You were programmed to detect any intrusion beyond the force field but you are malfunctioning due to short-circuits during a recent electrical storm. Your creators are large, segmented, warm-blooded, centipede-like bugs. Thus, as long as all the earthlings make physical contact with one another when they are beyond the force field your sensors will read them as one body and you will not activate.

- Contact is made with the force field anywhere from the top down. Note that prisoners are most likely to cross the plane of the force field from below, with their feet and legs.

- Contact is made with any part of the trees, posts, or other structure that borders the force field.

It is your judgment as a robot that determines whether or not you have been activated. You may want to confer with a fellow robot if you are unsure about a close call.

You can be deactivated for 5 minutes at a time if a prisoner points at you and says "a four-letter word."

You understand the prisoners but cannot speak. Should they ask you what they did to activate you, ignore them as you do not want to facilitate their escape.

13

Bomb Squad

Summary   A team must remove bombs that saboteurs have planted in the reactor room of a nuclear power station. The scenario is structured so that their best chance of success involves them all learning the system for safely removing the bombs and then each one taking a separate route to the power station.

Objectives   To explore team learning, creative problem solving, decision making, risk taking, and leadership.

Materials

1. Ten filled water balloons in a large paper shopping-bag.

2. One pair of large fireplace gloves.

3. One 10-sided die.

4. Ten large tin canisters. Remove one lid and the label from each. They must be large enough to hold the water balloons.

5. A length of rope to mark the boundaries of the nuclear reactor room.

6. A steel barrel to start a fire in and (optional) a cherry bomb, block buster, or other loud fireworks.*

Time Limit   35-60 minutes.

Procedure

1. Lay out the tin canisters as shown in Figure 8. Space the cans about 3 feet apart.

2. Place one water balloon in each can. Then put the fireplace gloves in the bag and leave the bag in the room.

3. Create the outline of a small room with the rope. Keep the rope about a 3 feet from any can and leave an open space with an end of the rope standing out to represent the door.

4. Prepare the fire in a nearby barrel. It will be lit later.

5. Take the group to a place near, but out of sight of, the tin cans. Briefly describe the activity and ask for volunteer observers. Ideally there should

* **Note:** Check state and local ordinances, as fireworks may be illegal in some areas.

be nine or ten members of the bomb squad. One or two more makes the task easier in some ways, while less than nine makes solving the problem harder.

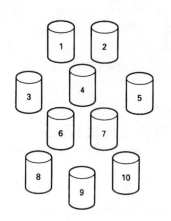

Figure 8. Bomb Squad.

6. Instruct the volunteers as to what specifics you want them to be watching for during the exercise.

7. Give the bomb squad the information given on Handout 13.1.

8. When the group is ready to go through the tunnels, ask who is going through how many different tunnels. For each different tunnel selected, the individual or group chooses three numbers and then throws the die. In order for them to elude the terrorists and get to the room, one of the numbers chosen must come up. If no one's number comes up, either they have failed in their mission or you may ask them to choose a different number from 1–10 and line up accordingly. They then throw the die three times to indicate who gets to the reactor room. Three 9s would mean that only the person who chose 9 would get there.

9. Take the group to the nuclear reactor room. Tell those who succeeded to stand outside the door and those who didn't to stand opposite them and outside the room. Remind those who did not make it that they may not communicate in any way with the survivors. Remind the bomb squad that communication is impossible between the reactor room and the outside. Tell the observers to close the rope door once one or more have entered.

10. While they are trying to deactivate the bomb, light the fire. Should they burst a balloon or exceed the time limit, you have the option of tossing a cherry bomb into the fire to signify the explosion.

11. If the group retrieves all the balloons from the nuclear reactor room, ask them to give them to you for verification. You can now slip the fireworks into the bag. Wrap the bag into a neat package and tell the participants to choose someone to toss the bag into the incinerator. If you use fireworks of any sort, emphasize the need to toss the bag in from 3 feet away and then move back quickly.

12. Conduct a review.

Commentary

This is an absorbing and challenging activity that demonstrates the importance and difficulty of system-wide learning. It can lead to discussions of how real work teams and organizations miss opportunities because knowledge, expertise, or information is not distributed throughout the system. The activity illustrates the paradox of how the measure of a truly integrated and functioning team is the ability of subgroups and individual members to carry out the team's mission alone and independently.

Another important area for discussion is the matter of chance and how it helps and hinders all team efforts. An offshoot of this subject is the danger of over-valuing and/or scapegoating individuals or subgroups for results that are often largely the product of uncontrolled and uncontrollable circumstances. Finally, this activity can lead to an unsuccessful conclusion. Thus it is a good one to use either early on to illustrate the challenges of teamwork or, in the later stages of a program, to measure progress. In either case, discussions of how teams handle failure and maintain morale can be fruitful.

Variations

The activity can be varied by making it easier.

1. One easier variation involves allowing the bomb squad to use items on their person and/or in their environment to assist with the solution.

2. Another is to tell them they must each choose a separate tunnel.

3. A third is to allow communication with those outside the room.

As much of the drama of this exercise depends on a credible scenario, try to keep believable any simplifications you make within the framework of the situation.

Instructions for the Bomb Squad

You are an elite bomb squad. Your mission is to neutralize a number of bombs that have been set in the reactor room of an abandoned nuclear power station by terrorists. If these bombs detonate, a serious meltdown will occur. A spy we planted in the terrorist group has provided the following information:

1.   Explosives have been placed inside ten canisters which are arranged in this pattern:

```
      1   2
    3   4   5
      6   7
    8   9    10
```

2.   In order to neutralize them, the explosives must be removed one at a time from their canisters as follows: first remove one explosive and place it in your bomb-bag; the empty can allows the others to be removed by being jumped Chinese-checker style until there is only one explosive left; that explosive may then be removed.

You may only jump if the canisters form straight lines (for example, cannister 9 can jump to cannister 5). An example of the process would be to put the explosive in canister 5 in the bag, then place the bomb in canister 3 in canister 5 and put the explosive in canister 4 in the bag.

The bomb has been wired to explode automatically if either of the following occurs:

(a)   The neutralization sequence described above is done improperly. There are no second chances.

(b)   One of the detonators explodes because it bursts open. Contact with oxygen will trigger an explosion.

These are time bombs in that they contain internal chemicals that will cause them to burst and explode within an approximate time span. Thus you must dispose of the bag with all the bombs in a nearby bomb-proof incinerator.

Instructions for the Bomb Squad (continued)

In your haste you all left immediately after you put on your camouflaged one-piece overalls and removed your jewelry. You have nothing in your pockets. You are in a large underground cave that is connected by tunnels to the power station. The whole underground system is made up of bare concrete walls and hard-packed dirt floors with not so much as a stone in them. From this point on there are ten different tunnel routes that lead to the reactor room. Seven of them are known to the terrorists and booby-trapped in such a manner that anyone using them is certain to be captured. We don't know which ones are guarded.

Once you are ready to take to the tunnels, notify the facilitator who will then tell you how to determine whether or not you make it to the reactor room. The room can only be opened from the outside and the door closes automatically once someone enters. Others may look in through the one-way mirror. Those inside the room will not be able to see outside or hear through the sound-proof walls. Our spy left the gloves which must be worn while handling the explosives inside a bomb-bag that is in the reactor room.

Reproduced from *CHANGING PACE Outdoor Games for Experiential Learning* by Carmine M. Consalvo, HRD Press, 1996

14

A Knotty Problem

Summary   Two or more teams of eight or ten form a circle and entangle themselves by joining hands and then attempt to disentangle the knot they are in without letting go.

Objectives   This classic activity is particularly relevant to issues of teamwork, leadership, and communication.

Materials   None.

Time Limit   30–60 minutes, depending on how many groups participate.

Procedure   1. Divide the group into equal teams of eight or ten. Use any extra people as observers. See the "Variations" section for an effective way to compare leadership processes using these extras.

2. Ask each group to form a tight circle. Once this is done tell them to join right hands with someone across from, not adjacent to, them. Emphasize that they must not clasp hands with someone adjacent to them at any time. Once right hands are clasped, instruct them to join left hands with a different person who is also opposite and not adjacent to them.

3. When all hands are clasped, tell participants that they need to do a test to ensure that they are properly joined. The test involves one person taking the lead by gently squeezing their right hand. The person whose hand is squeezed should then squeeze their left hand. The next person whose hand is squeezed should do likewise until everyone's hand has been squeezed. Inform participants that the squeeze test has failed if anyone's hand is not squeezed. In that eventuality, the team must release hands and begin again because once they untangled they would have formed two connected rings rather than one large circle.

4. When everyone has passed the squeeze test, tell participants their goal is to untangle themselves, forming a large circle without unclasping hands. Note that it is all right if some are facing in while others are facing out of the circle, and to alter the grip to improve comfort.

5. When everyone is ready, tell them to begin.

6. When all the groups have succeeded, conduct a review. Some groups need a long time and if your schedule is tight you may have to end the activity before they have finished.

Commentary

Teams naturally tend to view the task as a competition yet, despite equal size, no two knots—like no two problems—are the same. This activity nicely illustrates how other people's success cannot be duplicated by doing exactly what they did. The nature of both the problem and the team are different and in this activity the team members and the problem are, literally, closely intertwined. You will find many parallels with real teamwork situations by asking participants to describe what they had to do to succeed. Responses such as "twist myself around," "lead or wait depending on where I was positioned," and "be careful to let the person next to me know what I was going to do" are some of the many observations that can be transferred to team problem solving on the job.

Variations

1. One group can do the activity, but note that teams of 12 are unwieldy and the challenge is more difficult.

2. Groups can be divided between those that do and those that do not have an outside leader if *assigned* versus *emergent* leadership dynamics are of interest. In this case the observer is the leader. With this approach issues arise such as the degree to which the leader was followed and comparative ones such as how it felt to be in the different teams.

15

Zoo Parade

Summary   Teams of 8–10 must form a marching order according to size based on the animal that each participant is assigned. The task must be done while blindfolded and using only their animal's sound.

Objectives   This activity is conducive to in-depth discussions of ambiguity, uncertainty, risk taking, and trust as they relate to communication.

Materials
1. A set of 8–10 index cards for each team. Print one animal name on each card so that each set includes 8–10 different animals. Use animals of various sizes who make distinctive sounds, such as snake, lion, gorilla, cow, dog, cat, elephant, owl, monkey, duck, donkey, pig, crow, horse, mouse, chicken, rooster, lamb, bird, and wolf.

2. Bandannas for blindfolds are optional.

Time Limit   20-40 minutes, depending on group size.

Procedure
1. Divide the group into approximately equal teams of 8–10.

2. Explain that the goal is to form a marching order according to size, from largest to smallest, based on the animal that each participant will be assigned. Their constraints are that they are blind and the only sound they can make is that of their animal. Once they believe they are properly arranged, they are to march slowly as a unit for 10 feet.

3. Tell participants that they may peek if they must, but they must do so discreetly. See the "Materials" and "Procedure" sections of **Blind Faith** (game 3) if you are using blindfolds.

4. When everyone is ready, give each a card and tell them to think about the animal's size and sound and return the card to you quickly without letting anyone else see it.

5. When all the cards have been returned, announce the start of the exercise. Tell participants that you will watch out for their safety and ask them to move slowly and deliberately at all times.

6. Tell participants that when the march ends they regain sight and discuss with their team the feelings and difficulties associated with the task.

7. When all the teams have finished and the last team has had a couple of minutes' discussion, review with all the teams.

Commentary　　The ambiguity connected with varying interpretations of words such as "dog" and "snake" combined with the strong feelings this activity sometimes engenders can open the door to a profound appreciation of the need to be precise and descriptive in defining terms such as goals and vision. This exercise can produce enormous python snakes, cows that are barely 3 feet high, and an amazing respect for the need to assume nothing in important communications.

Variation　　A good way to vary this activity is to compare and contrast the differing interpretations that people assign to animals during the review. Comparing the same animal between groups leads to interesting disparities. Ask about interpretations of an animal's temperament to illustrate how prior experiences or lack thereof lead to divergent perceptions of many subjects.

16

Alphabet Soup

Summary A team tries to run its client through a maze of dots, representing a bureaucratic system, in as fast a time as possible.

Objectives To explore teamwork, goal setting, and customer service.

Materials
1. Plastic lids, or other round shape coffee or tennis ball cans, or other canisters. Have 15 of one color and 11 of another.

2. Enough rope or powdered lime to create a circle with a radius 13 feet and a starting line of 13 feet.

Time Limit 20-45 minutes.

Procedure
1. Print the letters, A, E, F, H, I, K, L, M, N, T, V, W, X, Y, and Z on the lids of one color using only straight lines. Print the remaining letters of the alphabet, B, C, D, G, J, O, P, Q, R, S, and U on the lids of the other color. Print these letters using curved lines.

2. With the rope or powdered lime make the circle with a radius of 13 feet and put A, E, I, O, and U at the center. Place the remaining letters randomly around the circle trying to keep adjacent letters at a distance from each other.

3. Pace off 26-33 feet from the circle and create the starting line.

4. Begin behind the starting line with a group of 8–16 participants. Give them the following instructions:

"Your goal is to get your client through the circular bureaucratic maze of dots lettered from A to Z in as fast a time as possible. Each dot represents a bureaucratic office. The letter is the office's acronym. Single-letter acronyms were instituted to simplify the bureaucracy. The bureaucratic system requires that these offices be contacted alphabetically beginning with A and ending with Z. The time begins when one of you steps over the line and ends when you are all back behind the starting line.

"One of you must volunteer to be the client. The client is the only one allowed in the circular system and he or she contacts each office by touching it."

"As is the case with most bureaucracies, this circular one has a pattern which was originally designed to serve its administrators. If you knew what the pattern was it might make your task easier.

"You have all the information you need. You may plan as long as you like."

5. When participants have succeeded once, ask them to set a time-limit goal before trying it again. Participants are not allowed to go to the circle or study it between attempts.

6. Each time they meet their goal, ask participants if they think they can improve their time.

7. They have finished when there is a consensus that the client has been through the maze as quickly as possible. The team can substitute clients. Ask participants if they want to know how long top-notch teams take to get their client through and, if they do, tell them "under one minute."

8. Conduct a review, and ask the client what team behavior helped, what didn't, and why. Also ask if anyone noted the pattern.

Commentary

This is a lively activity that can easily engage teams in meaty discussions of goal setting and customer service.

Variations

1. Let participants find out themselves that the sequence is alphabetical.

2. Use numbers instead of letters and place odd numbers opposite even numbers.

3. Add letters.

4. Create words.

17

Heroes, Heroines and Healers

Summary   A team tag game played with a ball and involving strategy.

Objectives   To explore teamwork, planning, and implementation, and to provide an energy boosting activity.

Materials
1. Two balls for each participant. The balls must be soft enough not to hurt should they inadvertently hit someone in the face. The ideal ball is called a "sensory" ball and is made from a light shiny plastic. Hundreds of them are used in amusement areas to create an effect like a swimming pool for children. The advantage the sensory ball has over other sponge balls is that it has a good throwing feel as well as a soft impact.

2. Enough rope or powdered lime to create a 12- foot boundary line.

Time Limit   15–30 minutes.

Procedure
1. Bring a group of 8–20 participants to a flat open area and divide them into two equal teams. Use an observer if you have an extra person.

2. Make a boundary line and have teams take opposite sides.

3. Give each team twice as many balls as there are members and give the following instructions:

> "This is a tag game played with a ball in which the goal is to eliminate the other team. If you are hit you are eliminated and cannot move from your place until the game is over. At the end of these instructions, you will have 5 minutes to determine the distribution of the balls and select two people to be given special abilities. The special ability of heroes and heroines is that they need to be hit three times before they can be eliminated; healers' special ability is to bring someone back to life by laying their hands on them. You can have any combination of the two. You may retrieve balls. Stay behind the boundary line at all times. Avoid high throws. Hitting anyone on the head does not count and may cause serious injury!"

4. Take questions and begin the 5-minute planning phase.

5. When the 5 minutes is up, tell participants that they have 5–10 minutes to eliminate the other team. If neither team is eliminated, the team with the most people alive at the end will be declared the winner.

6. Announce that the activity has started.

7. If there is sufficient time, energy, and interest, have a rematch.

8. When the activity is over, conduct a review.

Commentary

This is a quick and easy energizer that can promote planning strategy and tactical implementation that lends itself well to sophisticated discussions. Playing two rounds or the best three out of five mirrors real-world adjustments that planners have to make in order to adapt to unexpected contingencies in the implementation stage. The advantages of heroes and heroines who add *resistance* to a system versus healers who add *resilience* can be an interesting review topic as these attributes relate to planning and other aspects of the group's work.

Variations

1. Four teams can play by making two boundary lines in the form of the letter X. This version can be wild and mirrors the chaos of the real world where competitors are numerous.

2. Adding the option of one extra ball per person for each specialized person not used complicates the strategic possibilities.

18

Contortions and Gyrations

Summary   Two teams compete to be the first to keep three balls simultaneously off the ground for 5 seconds without using their arms or hands. The team playing the best two rounds out of three wins.

Objectives   To explore teamwork, planning versus doing, provide an energy boost and have fun.

Materials   1. Six 20-inch inflated beach balls. You may want to underinflate one or two to make the task easier.

2. Two stopwatches.

Time Limit   20–40 minutes.

Procedure

1. Put the two groupings of three beach balls a few inches apart from each other.

2. Outline the activity and ask for volunteer referee/timekeepers. You will need at least one referee/timekeeper, and ideally you will have two or more. Divide the remainder of your group into two equal teams of four or five.

3. Explain that the winners will have to win two out of three rounds. In the first round the first team to keep all three balls suspended off the ground for 5 seconds, without using their hands or arms, is the winner.

4. Instruct the referee/timekeepers, to watch for hand or arm violations, and give them stopwatches. If there is only one referee you will have to be the other.

5. Announce the start of the first round.

6. At the end of the first round, if participants had great difficulty in round one, under-inflate the balls a little. Inform participants that the second round is the same as the first except that only two participants from each team must now keep the three balls off the ground. Team members without the balls can help as long as they do not give any physical assistance. Players can switch places with teammates in either direction at any time.

7. At the end of the second round, if the score is one to one, repeat round one or two depending on how each went and time constraints.

8. Conduct a review and discussion.

Commentary This activity can be quite challenging. It gives rise to interesting discussions about the advantages and disadvantages of taking action quickly and adapting and improvising along the way versus pausing at the outset to plan a systematic approach and ensure full input. Either approach can succeed in this exercise if done well. Trial and error without blame, and flexibility, are essential to success whatever the approach.

Variation Use four balls in the third round and let the whole team try to keep them off the ground. This can be a stimulating activity for as many as 50 participants.

19

Embrace

Summary   A tag energizer in which you can avoid being tagged if you are embracing someone else.

Objectives   To explore team building and provide an energy boost.

Materials   1. A bean bag or other soft throwing object that does not roll.

2. One to four boundary ropes 30–50 feet long.

Time Limit   10–15 minutes.

Procedure   1. Find a flat open area. Using natural boundaries and one or more ropes, create a playing field 60–120 square yards depending on the size and athleticism of the group.

2. Tell the group that the person who is "it" has the ball and can make others "it" by hitting them with it. If you are in the embrace of someone else, you cannot become "it" unless your hug exceeds the 4-second limit. (Determine 4 seconds by counting 1001, 1002, 1003, 1004.) When the rope boundaries begin to shrink the field, tags must be made by hand rather than with the ball. If you step out of bounds you are automatically "it."

3. Note that anyone who wants to can help with the ropes. This option allows anyone who has discomfort with the activity, or is unable to participate, to opt out.

4. Ask for a volunteer to be "it" and begin.

5. After 5 minutes, or when you feel there needs to be a change in the action, move one of the ropes inward. Continue shrinking the playing-field until you are ready to end the activity.

Commentary   This activity can energize any size of group but should be used with those who have already completed several team-building activities involving physical contact.

Variation   Once the hand tags begin, those participants who are tagged become helpers, and the game ends when everyone is "it."

20

Blob Tag

Summary	A tag game for any size group in which each person tagged joins hands with the others until everyone is "it".
Objectives	To explore teamwork and provide an energizer.
Materials	One to four boundary ropes 35–50 feet long.
Time Limit	15–20 minutes.
Procedure	1. Find a flat open area and, using natural boundaries and one or more ropes, create a playing field of 120 square yards or more depending on the size and athleticism of the group.
	2. Tell the group that the Blob is a game in which those tagged become helpers and the game ends when everyone is "it." The Blob grows from the first person who is "it" to everyone because each person tagged joins hands with the tagger. A tag can only be made by the free hands of the two end people. The Blob can spontaneously split off in order to tag someone. Once there are two Blobs, both can tag individuals. Once all the individuals are gone, the largest Blob goes after the smaller one. If both Blobs are equal, both Blobs win.
	3. Take questions and ask for a volunteer to be "it".
	4. When the activity ends, conduct a review.
Commentary	This exercise is a lighthearted way to begin talking about what consti tutes being a team and how it is different from operating as an indi vidual. If the Blob splits, ask how that happened and what its effects were in terms of teamwork. The split creates competition. Usually internal co-operation and teamwork intensify once there is another Blob to compete against. Also ask how teamwork and the sense of being a team changed as the size of the Blob increased.
Variations	1. The Blob makes a good 5- to 10- minute energizer if you omit the review.
	2. The split can be eliminated or used by the Blob in order to tag someone without creating another Blob. No splitting makes the game last longer, while splitting makes it end sooner.

21

You're Fantastic!

Summary

A walking tag game in which the person tagged is told "you're fantastic!" and she or he then spins around three times saying "Isn't that marvelous!" at each spin.

Objectives

To break the ice and energize.

Materials

One to four boundary-line ropes 35–50 feet long.

Time Limit

10–15 minutes.

Procedure

1. Find a flat, open area and, using natural boundaries and one or more ropes, create a playing area of 60 square yards or more depending on the size of the group.

2. Tell the group that the next activity is a new kind of tag game. Rather than running, they must walk. And rather than being dehumanized by being called "it," the person tagged is told "You're fantastic!" and he or she then spins around three times saying "Isn't that marvelous!" at each spin. Another civilizing factor in this game is the rule that whenever anyone accidentally bumps into someone, the offender must catch up with the person and say "So sorry!" three times while making an exaggerated apologetic gesture of his/her choice. The person apologized to must respond with "Thank you! Thank you! Thank you!" while adopting an extremely grateful posture.

3. Take questions and ask for a volunteer to be "fantastic."

4. End the activity while the energy and laughter is still high.

Commentary

This is primarily a lighthearted activity to be introduced early on in the program with large or small groups.

Variations

1. You can substitute other words such as *awesome, sensational, excellent,* and *outstanding.*

2. You can also make it a name game by having participants say "You're fantastic (Charles)!" and "Isn't that marvelous (Mary)!"

22

Ball and Chain

Summary   A relay race in which groups of three are joined by a rope at their belt loops. There are several ways of winning.

Objectives   To explore teamwork and goals.

Materials   1. A rope at least 30 feet long for each triad.

2. A inexpensive carabiner for each triad. Key ring carabiners or even large key rings or binder rings can be substituted.

3. Two lengths of rope to designate the starting and finishing lines.

4. Pairs of brightly-colored shorts in a variety of sizes or ropes that are at least 30 feet long so that they can be tied around participants' waists.

Time Limit   20–30 minutes.

Procedure   1. Ascertain who doesn't have belt loops and either appoint them as judges or provide them with shorts or longer ropes before going to the race site.

2. Place the starting and finishing lines anywhere from 65 to 100 feet apart depending on the athleticism of the group.

3. Briefly describe the race and ask for judges. Those with physical handicaps should be the first choices for judges.

4. Divide the remainder of the group into triads.

5. Give each triad a length of rope and a carabiner.

6. Instruct participants with the carabiners to clip them to a belt-loop at the back of a teammate's trousers.

7. Tell participants to run the rope through the carabiner and attach the two ends to the belt-loops (or waists) of the two other team members. All three should all be hooked into each other, with the person with the carabiner being able to move anywhere along the rope and the other two fixed at the opposite ends of it.

8. Once participants are properly connected, have each triad stretch the rope taut between them. Then ask them to line up parallel to the starting line. Note that there will be three laps, which will allow each person to be in the middle.

9. Before signaling the start of the first race, list the following ways of winning:

   a.   the first person on your team to cross the finish line

   c.   the first team whose member crosses the finish line

   d.   the team to accumulate the most points over the three rounds

10. Five team points will be awarded to the team whose member crosses the line first and ten team points will go to the team that crosses first. Note that the judges' primary responsibility will be to declare the first person and first team across the line and to tabulate team scores and announce the winners.

11. Signal the start of the first round.

12. At the end of each round the judges declare the winners and announce team scores while teams rearrange themselves to put a new person in the middle.

13. At the end of the third round applaud the winners and/or give them a prize and conduct a review and discussion.

Commentary

This exercise is especially helpful in sparking discussion of co-operation versus competition, interdependence, and individual versus team goals. Both the multiple goals and interdependent structure of the triads make this activity particularly relevant to the notion of "co-opetition." Co-opetition combines the competitive as well as the co-operative nature of teamwork in a manner which directs individual competitiveness toward team and personal goals. It accepts individual competitiveness and rewards and channels it in co-operative directions rather than denying, ignoring, or condemning it.

Variation

Reverse all the ways of winning so that coming in last is the goal. This approach is less strenuous and can also be used as the second round to give participants a rest. In this version, stopping results in a disqualification.

23

Creative Connections

Summary   Each participant is given an index card with the name of a man-made object on it. On the signal they pair up and try to make connections and/or inventions based on the objects on their two cards. They have 40 seconds before they start again by forming a new dyad.

Objectives   To explore creativity and provide an ice-breaker and energy-booster.

Materials   1. Index cards (3" x 5") bearing the names of fabricated objects, such as a, telephone, fishing-rod, fax machine, doorbell, shovel, outhouse, pencil sharpener, food processor, zipper, lawn mower, answering machine, computer, hair-dryer, dentist's chair, escalator, bathtub, crystal ball, can opener, wrench, video camera, stethoscope, mouse trap, fire extinguisher, fan, trampoline, jacuzzi, drill, pogo-stick, umbrella, blowtorch, stapler, and so on.

2. A whistle may be necessary for larger groups so that the signal can be heard.

Time Limit   20–40 minutes, depending on group size and the number of rounds you run.

Procedure   1. Pass the cards around face down and ask participants to take one without looking at it first.

2. Inform the group that creativity often involves forced connections between seemingly disparate objects and/or ideas. Tell participants that in this game they will pair up with someone else and try to create connections and/or inventions based on the two words they have. For example, if they have "water faucet" and "flashlight," one connection is that they both deal with flow, another is they could be combined to create a flashlight that doubled as a canteen, and a third is the idea of a battery-operated car that consumes water so that water stations would replace gas stations. Note that these connections range from simple relationships to realistic combinations to more tangential and less feasible inventions.

3. Tell participants that all associations are acceptable as the purpose is to stretch their thinking, not to produce a patentable invention, since they will have only 40 seconds before you signal them to pair up with someone new to try to make connections and/or inventions based on that person's object.

4. Signal the start and re-signal every 40 seconds until everyone has paired with everyone else or enough time has been spent.

5. Ask participants to share any connections that were particularly creative or funny.

Commentary This is a good exercise for large groups and/or groups who are getting to know each other.

Variation You can use this activity as a name game. Ask participants to exchange names using alliteration (for example, Jumping John or Merry Mary) before they make their connections. John and Mary ask each other their names by saying "jumping" and "merry." If either doesn't remember the other's name, they are told again.

24

Silent Hug

Summary	A closing activity in which the group forms a circle and everyone hugs everyone else without speaking.
Objectives	To explore team building and bring closure to an activity.
Materials	None.
Time Limit	Approximately 10 minutes for the game and a total of 20–30 minutes if you do a review.
Procedure	1. Gather the group in a circle at the end of a program and invite participants to share their observations and feelings. When that process feels complete, note that the last activity involves a non-verbal way to close the circle and the day.
	2. Explain that participants will turn and hug the person on their immediate left and then the person next to them, and so on around the circle. Note that the first person a participant hugged follows behind you and also hugs the person on their left who hugs the person to their left, and so on down the line so that everyone hugs every one else once.
Commentary	This activity can be quite moving when carried out with a group that is beginning to feel close. It will not *create* that closeness and so should be used with discrimination. There will always be the occasional person who feels uncomfortable with this exercise and it is not one such people can easily decline to do.
Variation	This activity can be simply a closing hug in which you note that speaking is optional.

25

The Great Escape

Summary   A group of space explorers is held prisoner in a cell made out of high-voltage wires. They all need to escape over the electric walls because everyone is needed to navigate their spacecraft.

Objectives   To explore teamwork and problem solving.

Materials   1. A 130–200 foot length of rope.

2. 2 x 8 inch or 2 x 10 inch plank 8 or 9 feet long.

Time Limit   45–75 minutes.

Procedure   1. Find three or four trees in a private area and wrap the rope around them to create the cell. Take the following into consideration in making the prison:

   a.   Vary the heights of each side such that the flattest, safest, and most obstacle-free side will be the one chosen because it is the lowest and easiest route to cross.

   b.   Angle the tops of the walls with the easy wall nearly parallel to the ground.

   c.   The wall height should be approximately half the length of the plank, and never so low that a participant could step over it.

   d.   The side of the cell that will be crossed must be longer than the plank.

   e.   Place the plank inside the prison. It should fit easily.

2. Briefly describe the activity and ask for volunteer observers who will call any violations of the electrical field and note how the team works together. Give those with bad ankles, backs, knees, etc. first preference to be observer/judges. The team of prisoners should be between 6 and 12.

3. Ask the group to enter the cell and tell them the following:

   "You are a group of space explorers held captive by the invisible aliens that inhabit this planet. The walls of your cell are made from high-voltage wires. The electrical field runs down to the ground and through the trees. All materials conduct this alien electricity. You use the plank in your cell to receive food. If anything contacts the electric field a signal alerts the aliens who then re-imprison anyone outside the cell. You all need to escape because everyone is needed to navigate your spacecraft.

"While you are encouraged to be creative and experimental in your attempted escapes anything deemed unsafe will not be allowed. For instance, you may not leap, dive, or catapult over the wall because of the danger of turning an ankle, or worse. Good luck, space travelers! You have 30–40 minutes before the aliens will be taking you to a more secure prison."

4. When they are all out or the time is up, conduct a review.

Commentary

This classic outdoor activity provides an excellent team challenge. However it requires extra attention to safety in order to avoid falls and ankle sprains. Be ready to break an accidental fall as participants are lifted over the wall. Instruct observers to do the same. Using a safe site in terms of level ground and soft, sure footing where participants will land is important.

Variation

Make one wall drop steeply so that the side adjacent to the easy wall is the lowest of the cell. This low spot should be just large enough for one small person and be the best place for the last person to escape using the plank. Again, ensure good footing around this area.

26

Marooned

Summary   To achieve their separate goals, two unrelated groups must assist each other in crossing a river.

Objectives   To explore teamwork and collaboration between teams. This activity dramatically illustrates how trust and co-operation between teams can enable them to accomplish otherwise impossible tasks.

Materials

1. Two hardwood loading pallets of the type used to haul and load heavy materials such as bricks using a fork lift. Each should be large enough to hold your group of 8–12 participants. They should be approximately the same size and range from 30–55 square feet. Nail boards perpendicular to the pallet slats to create a platform leaving no spaces between the boards. Spaces are a hazard as participants might trip on them.

2. Two 2 x 10 inch planks that are 10–12 feet long.

3. A nearly-full bucket of water dyed red with food coloring.

Time Limit   40–60 minutes.

Procedure

1. Place the two platforms so that the distance between them is 30–40 inches less than the combined length of the two planks. The following explanation of the solution will help you gauge the ideal distance that should be determined by experimentation.

Solution:
The planks should be sufficiently far apart so that jumping from one to the other results in a plank hitting the ground and thus being weakened by the river. The only way to get across should involve one team giving its plank to the other. Then both planks should be made to span the river in the following manner. One plank is counterbalanced by two or more people while another person goes out on it carrying the other plank. The other plank then rests on the first board and the opposite platform to create a bridge. Approximately 2 inches on each end of the second board are needed to make a secure bridge. The amount of plank that is needed to counterbalance the weight of the participant plus the plank depends on the length and flexibility of the planks. The shorter and more rigid the planks the further apart the platforms can be.

2. Put one plank on each platform. Place the bucket of red liquid on one of the platforms.

3. Briefly describe the activity and ask for volunteers to observe and judge whether or not the planks touch the river.

4. Divide the rest of the group into two approximately equal teams of 4–6 participants.

5. Give one team a natives information sheet (Handout 26.1) and the other an anthropologists information sheet (Handout 26.2). Send the anthropologists to the platform with the liquid and the natives to the other platform.

6. Announce that the activity is underway and note that participants have 25–40 minutes to cross.

7. Conduct a review when the time is up.

Commentary   The fact that neither group can accomplish its task unless one team surrenders its resources (the plank) makes for a particularly compelling activity that demonstrates the need for trust and collaboration to achieve goals that are otherwise impossible. The fragility of trust between groups with different functions or cultures arises out of the conflicting views that each holds regarding the red liquid. The anthropologists sometimes distrust the natives' claim that the liquid is toxic even though they have no information indicating that the natives are untrustworthy.

Variations   1. A simpler version starts with all the participants and both planks on the same platform.

2. A variation that requires a more complicated solution informs the anthropologists that the natives are not to be trusted around the healing liquid. They are told never to hand the liquid to the natives or allow themselves to be outnumbered by them when they are holding it.

Marooned
Natives Information Sheet

A typhoon has washed out the bridge and you are stranded on what is left of it. You are a group of natives who inadvertently drank a life-threatening red liquid. You have traveled here to find the shaman who is known to be able to cure those who drink this toxic liquid. He lives in the mountains across the river. You must get there soon or perish.

The river water has strange corrosive properties that make swimming impossible. If the plank were to contact the water more than twice, it would no longer be able to hold a person's weight.

Marooned
Anthropologists Information Sheet

A typhoon has washed out the bridge and you are stranded on what is left of it. You are a group of medical anthropologists who must cross the river in order to rendezvous with the supply helicopter which is due today. It will not be back again for another 10 days. You cannot wait. You lost all your food during the typhoon. The wildlife and plants that exist in this area are minimal and potentially lethal.

Your original mission was to find a shaman who is famous for his healing powers. You succeeded. Although communication was difficult, you gathered that his healing powers are related to the red liquid you have brought back with you. If you don't obtain new food supplies you may have to drink the healing potion, which can potentially make you all rich and famous.

The river water has strange corrosive properties that makes swimming impossible. If the plank were to contact the water more than twice, it would no longer be able to hold a person's weight.

27

Scarlet Letters

Summary   Each member of a group of 25 or more is given an index card with a black letter on one side and a red (scarlet) letter on the other. Their task is to create three-, four- and five-letter words. Every 30–60 seconds participants group together in fours to form a different word using their letters. If they fail to form a word they are eliminated. The exercise ends when only one foursome remains.

Objectives   This is a large-group energizer that explores competition and team building.

Materials   1. Print large capital letters in scarlet or red on index cards. A set of 50 would have the following distribution: A(5), B(1), C(1), D(2), E(6), F(1), G(2), H(1), I(5), L(2), M(1), N(3), O(4), P(1), R(3), S(2), T(3), U(2), V(1), W(1), X(1), Y(1) and one wild card with a dot (.) on it. On the backs of the cards write the same combination of letters in black ink, taking care not to create a card with two vowels, two wild cards, or a wild card and a vowel.

2. A stopwatch and a whistle.

3. Scrabble™ dictionary to verify words.

4. Optional prizes for the winning group.

Time Limit   15–25 minutes.

Procedure   1. Hand out the cards.

2. Inform the group that they must pay strict attention as this activity requires them to remember the rules under stress. Note that each has a card with a black letter on one side and a scarlet letter on the other. Tell participants their task will be to create three-, four-, or five-letter words by grouping together every 30–60 seconds to form a different word that uses their letters. If they do not form a word, they are eliminated. All words must appear in the Scrabble™ dictionary to be accepted. The exercise ends when only one foursome remains. They will be the winners. If you are awarding prizes, tell them now.

3. Note that three-letter words can be formed by black letters only and four-letters words can be formed by scarlet letters only, while five-letter words must be formed by a combination of black and scarlet letters. A dot on the

card means it is a wild card which can be used as any consonant *but not as a vowel*. Repeat this rule and ask if all are clear before continuing.

4. Tell them that whenever they hear your whistle (demonstrate) they must listen carefully as the number of blows signals the number of letters in the next word.

5. Note that they will have between 30 and 60 seconds to form a word. You can use 30, 45, and 60 seconds to correspond to three-, four-, and five-letter words, or you can vary the timing as you please.

6. When all the participants are ready, blow your whistle to begin. At the end of each sequence ask those who are "out" to help you verify that the words made are acceptable. Ask for a volunteer to use the Scrabble™ dictionary after the first round.

7. Continue until there is a winning team.

8. Review is optional.

Commentary

This is an effective energizer for 20 or more participants. It raises feelings about competition and transient teams that can be edifying. Conducting a review with more than 25 is awkward, however, unless you break the group into subgroups and, ideally, have co-facilitators to join with each. This activity can also be used with a large group and then discussed when participants break into smaller groups.

Telling the group that a valuable prize is involved can make the competition quite fierce. It also adds to the pandemonium that exists anyway. You may want an assistant if the group is larger than 50.

Variation

A simpler version uses one-sided cards or Scrabble™ pieces.

28

Applauding Differences

Summary   The group forms a circle and practices giving a rousing standing ovation. Then participants enter the circle and take a bow based on whatever distinction the facilitator or participants bring up. The distinctions can be as disparate as being born in another country, being an only child, or playing the piano.

Objectives   To explore an energizer that promotes discussion of team building, rewards, and cultural norms.

Materials   None.

Time Limit   15–25 minutes.

Procedure   1. Ask the group to form a circle. Note that building a positive team culture through norms, rewards, and celebrating differences is important to team building. Explain that this exercise is designed to establish and experience all three.

2. Tell participants that you want their team to establish a norm of providing as a reward clear and unequivocal applause whenever an individual or the team as a whole does well. Note that such norms are usually associated with high morale.

3. Begin by practicing a standing ovation. Ask participants to recall how they applauded a great play, musical event, or athletic performance. Tell them to exaggerate their clapping and add hoots and whistles to increase the volume.

4. After two or three rounds of applause, tell participants that appreciating diversity in a team is crucial to its success. Tell them that when you call out a distinction, such as "plays a musical instrument," all those to whom it applies should enter the circle and the others should applaud them loudly. The applauders should also call out the names of those in the circle to personalize the experience. Tell participants that they can also call out distinctions as the spirit moves them.

5. Begin calling out distinctions. The following examples are provided to demonstrate how varied the distinctions can be so as to stimulate your own ideas:

- Put shoes on by putting on a sock and a shoe and a sock and a shoe
- Begin showering by washing your hair
- Hardly ever shower
- Hardly ever take a bath
- Hardly ever take a bath or a shower
- Climb mountains
- Surf
- Hunt
- Fish
- Garden
- Have more than three brothers and sisters
- Have been to Africa
- Have changed careers
- Have been married over 10 years
- Have relatives in foreign countries
- Have a hobby that no one would guess
- Have a skill that no one would guess
- Have acted in a play
- Have performed on a stage
- Were college athletes
- Have painted or otherwise created something that is framed and hanging on a wall

6. End the applause while the group is still energetic.

7. Ask the group if the norm of applauding each other is one they want for their team. If it is, tell them you and any members of the group who act as observers will note whether and to what degree participants are keeping that norm.

8. Ask the group to select one other norm which will be treated similarly.

Commentary

This activity gets people acquainted, celebrates differences, and provides an effective way to introduce the role and importance of cultural norms in a team. It also establishes the norm of rewarding the good work of individuals and the team with a standing ovation, which is particularly helpful when introduced early in a program and then reinforced as it promotes a team spirit that improves both performance and morale.

Variations

1. With larger groups you can omit the creation of norms as it is too cumbersome.

2. Teams of 8–10 can spend considerable time exploring the issues of rewards, norms, and diversity by noting that different people prefer different kinds of rewards and norms. A good way to begin is to observe the fact that some people seemed to relish being applauded while others were indifferent or even a little uncomfortable.

29

Shuffling the Deck

Summary   A team or teams of eight have to rearrange themselves from one pattern to another according to a set of rules. One to four participants work on the same puzzle using coins. The team that finishes first offers to show the other team the solution.

Objectives   To explore teamwork between teams and leadership.

Materials

1. Each team of eight will need ten mats, rug samples, linoleum squares, or other material that can serve as markers and not blow away outdoors.

2. Eight coins.

3. Four bandannas for each team.

Time Limit   35–50 minutes.

Procedure

1. Place the ten markers in a row. If using multiple teams, each set should be out of immediate earshot and ideally out of sight of the others.

2. Briefly explain the activity and divide the group into one or more teams of eight and one team of 2–5. You can use one person if your numbers are limited. Observers are optional.

3. Give each team of eight four bandannas.

4. Take all the participants to a set of markers and provide the following instructions:

"Start with four people wearing bandannas on the first four markers and those without them on the adjacent four markers. Ask one team to arrange itself accordingly. There should be two empty markers at one end.

"The goal is to shuffle into an alternating pattern of bandannas/ none/bandannas/none/etc., or none/bandannas/none/ bandannas/ etc., as quickly and in as few moves as possible. Ask the same group to demonstrate the two solutions.

"The only restraint is that each move must involve two people moving simultaneously to the two open spaces. The simultaneous movement requirement means that the two people cannot change places with each other. They must always go to the two empty spaces that existed before either of them moved.

"All solutions must be verified by being demonstrated to the facilitator."

5. Give the small group the eight coins and tell them they can use them to solve the puzzle at the place you have pre-selected.

6. Instruct any additional teams to go to their markers. When all the participants are at their positions, tell them to begin and that they have 15–25 minutes to finish.

7. Verify solutions and then instruct the team to offer to help but not to insist on helping the other teams.

8. When the time is up or everyone has finished, ask who won. Note that all teams who reshuffled can be said to have won. Also note the order of completion and the number of moves each team made.

9. Conduct a review.

Commentary

This exercise is effective at promoting discussion about how teams relate with other teams. It illustrates the desire of groups to solve a problem on their own, how the same task can be structured differently, how teams resist leadership when it comes in the middle of a process, and how teams may value or attend to complex goals (that is, as fast and with as few moves) differently.

Variation

1. With two teams, one can have an outside leader who is allowed to use the coins and the teams can compare their experiences and performance.

2. The coins can be eliminated.

30

The *Titanic*

Summary
Two ships are sinking and there are a limited number of lifeboats available. To reach the shore passengers must squeeze together and create a ferry system. If the two ships share their lifeboats the task is easier, quicker, and safer for all.

Objectives
To explore team building, problem solving, and teamwork between teams.

Materials

1. Four pieces of rope, each approximately 33 feet long. Two ropes represent the sinking ships and two represent the shoreline.

2. Pieces of plywood or carpet, between 280–350 square feet each, to represent lifeboats. Carpet samples with sewn edges work well; outdated ones can be bought inexpensively from home decorators. The carpet pieces can vary both in size and shape or they can all be the same. You will need two pieces for each shipload of 4–9 participants.

Time Limit
35–50 minutes.

Procedure

1. Form ship-like shapes with two of the ropes. The "ships" should be about 13 feet apart. Place the two shoreline ropes about 40–50 feet across from each ship.

2. Put two pieces of plywood or carpet in each ship.

3. Briefly describe the activity and ask for at least one volunteer observer/judge for each ship. Tell them to note how their teams work together and to notify those who step or fall into the water that they have done so.

4. Divide the group into two equal teams and assign each to a ship.

5. Give the teams the following instructions:

   "You are a modern *Titanic* that is sinking fast because of damage by icebergs. You have 20-30 minutes before your ship goes down. The water is too cold to swim in. The ropes opposite you represent the safety of an island shore. The builders of your ship believed it was unsinkable and thus you have only two small lifeboats represented by the two pieces of wood or carpet. You must be standing entirely on one boat or another.

Observers are responsible for calling any missteps. Those who step or fall off must sail back to the ship for medical treatment for hypothermia.

"To sail your lifeboats, place one piece in front of the other and step on top of it. You may not throw your lifeboats at any time. Bon voyage!"

6. When they all arrive on shore or the time is up, conduct a review.

Commentary

It is remarkable how few teams collaborate to make the task considerably easier and survival more likely. More often the task is perceived as a competitive race even though it is about survival, not winning. Using this task early on can demonstrate the need for and relevance of working with rather than *apart from* or against other teams. Use late in a program to test how well the teams have progressed.

Variation

1. The Titanic is suitable for just one group. With 15 or more participants, use three ships. This approach makes collaboration even more profitable but also more difficult as all three have to surrender the competitive perspective which seems to get stronger as the number of teams increases.

2. With 20 participants use four groups of five.

31

Board Meeting

Summary   A team of participants tries to balance itself on a small board sufficiently long to sing the chorus of a song.

Objectives   To explore team size, team building, problem solving, creativity, and quality.

Materials   1. Three pieces of plywood each approximately 110, 145, and 220 square inches. The smallest will be used for teams of 6–8 and the largest for teams of 9–12 participants. The mid-sized board can be used to introduce a greater or lesser challenge at the outset or after a group has either succeeded or failed on the first board.

2. Create a platform under the plywood by nailing 2 x 4 inch studs around the four outside edges. The 2-inch wide space under the board makes the task more challenging.

Time Limit   40–60 minutes.

Procedure   1. If the group is large enough, divide participants into approximately equal teams. Briefly describe the activity and ask for one or two volunteer observers from each team to note teamwork, assist with breaking any falls, and watch for anyone touching the ground before the chorus is over. Try to keep the challenge levels the same for each team based on the numerical and physical size of each group and the size of its board.

2. Give each group a board and tell participants to balance themselves on it long enough to sing the chorus of a song.

3. Note that the chorus words are to be created by the team and adapted to the melody of their choice. The words should reflect a positive and realistic statement about the team's goals.

4. Tell participants that they have 20–35 minutes to complete their task.

5. Assist with ensuring that no one falls while attempting to balance.

6. Teams that finish ahead of time may try for a better-quality performance.

7. When all participants have accomplished the task or the time is up, conduct a review.

Commentary   This is a good opening exercise as it starts participants thinking about team goals. Quality can be examined from the point of view of touches, the song lyrics, the pace at which the song was sung, the stability of the team on the board, and the group's process in terms of full and frank discussion.

The activity is also a metaphor for meetings in which so many people are involved that the process is awkward and cumbersome. Boards are often so large that all meaningful business must take place in smaller committees. Teams are generally most effective when there are enough members to ensure diversity and yet not so many as to either prolong the process or promote domination by a few in the interest of efficiency. Five to nine participants make the best team size. Nine increases the chances of a rich mixture of ideas. Five is needed for a quorum.

Variation   1. After a team has had an initial success, they try a smaller, more challenging board. The review session concentrates on what, if any, changes occurred when the difficulty of the problem increased.

2. The activity can be run as a competition between teams of the same number using identical boards.

3. Boards of the same approximate size but different shapes can be used. Teams draw straws to see who picks first from a circle, square, triangle, or rectangle.

32

Water, Water, Everywhere

Summary

Using large buckets, a team has to fill to overflowing a large barrel which is riddled with holes. It must decide between (a) fewer holes or more buckets, (b) fewer limits on how it blocks the holes or less distance between the barrel and the water and, (c) more participating team members or more time.

Objectives

To explore teamwork, problem solving, planning, decision making, and energizing. [If tension has built between two teams during prior activities, collaborating on this one will bring them back together.]

Materials

1. A 55-gallon steel or plastic drum. Scatter 150 holes in the barrel using a spike which corresponds to an available cork size.

2. Two bags, each with 25 corks to fit the holes.

3. Four plastic buckets with capacities ranging from about 1 1/2–3 gallons. All but the largest should have handles.

4. A lake, ocean, river, well, spigot, or other abundant source of water.

Time Limit

50–75 minutes.

Procedure

1. Place the barrel 50–65 feet from the water source. Place the smallest bucket 13–20 feet from the water. This spot will be the alternative place for the drum.

2. Place the other buckets and the bags of corks next to the barrel.

3. Bring a team of 7–12 participants to the barrel and tell them their goal is to fill the barrel to overflowing. You should have given them prior notice to bring towels and to wear shoes and clothing which they do not mind getting wet. Give participants advance notice to wear shorts, bathing suits or sandals if appropriate.

4. Give participants the following instructions:

   "You have 15–20 minutes to decide on the parameters of this task based on the following options:

4. Give participants the following instructions:

"You have 15–20 minutes to decide on the parameters of this task based on the following options:

  a. You have four buckets and you can trade at the rate of one bucket for each bag of 25 corks. You can use the corks to plug up holes in the drum.

  b. You can leave the barrel where it is and use any part of your anatomy to block the holes or you can move the barrel to the spot where the small bucket is placed, but use only your hands, arms, feet, and legs to plug the holes.

Once you determine these options you will have 15 minutes to fill the barrel to overflowing. You can trade up to three team members at the rate of 5 minutes for each to increase the amount of time you have to complete the task. Those who opt out must do so willingly. They will serve as observers and comment on how the team performed at the review.

All these decisions must be made either by consensus or majority vote. Corks must be in place, the barrel moved, and observers selected before the 15-20 minutes are up."

5. When participants have implemented their decisions or the time is up, begin the barrel filling.

6. If the team is having problems, you can call a break and suggest that they might need more time, members, buckets, or corks. Leave it to the team to decide, based on consensus or majority vote, what they need, if anything, to complete the task.

7. When the time is up or they complete the task, conduct a review.

This is a light-hearted exercise in which participants directly experience the consequences of decisions. It is best used in warm weather and just before lunch or at the end of the day. Participants must be notified in advance of the nature of the exercise. Participants will need to change clothes.

1. Once you are familiar with the activity put a price on the buckets, corks, time, distance, and so on. Give participants a set amount of money based on your estimate of what should be enough. They then make their purchases.

2. Using two or more groups can turn this exercise into a sometimes hilarious competition. Pricing the items allows for cost-benefit comparisons after the competition.

33

Switch

Summary	A computer "glitch" makes it necessary for a team to improvise a way to switch the position of two energy orbs in order to avert an explosion that will be powerful enough to obliterate all trace of them and their spacecraft.
Objectives	To explore teamwork and creative problem solving.
Materials	1. Six large tins approximately 6 inches in diameter and 7 inches high. Remove one lid from each.
	2. Three inexpensive, lightweight balls about the size of a regulation volleyball. Each ball should sit snugly on top of the tin. Most of the ball should be exposed above the lid of the tin to make lifting the ball off its pedestal easy.
	3. A 115 foot or longer piece of 1–inch multipurpose utility rope.
	4. A 65–100 foot boundary rope.
	5. Two ropes or enough powdered lime to make circles 3 foot 4 inches in radius.
Time Limit	40–60 minutes.
Procedure	Refer to Figure 9 while following the instructions for the setup of the activity numbered 1–4 below.
	1. Outline an area 16 1/2 feet square using the boundary rope.
	2. Place two tins opposite each other and 3 feet 4 inches outside the roped-in area.
	3. Place two balls on top of the open ends of two tins and make a circle of 3 feet 4 inch radius around each tin using rope or lime.
	4. Put the 1–inch rope, the other ball, and the other four tins a few feet from one of the circled tins.
	5. Bring your group to the area. Briefly explain the task and ask for volunteer observer/judges. The team who switches the balls should have between five and eight members.

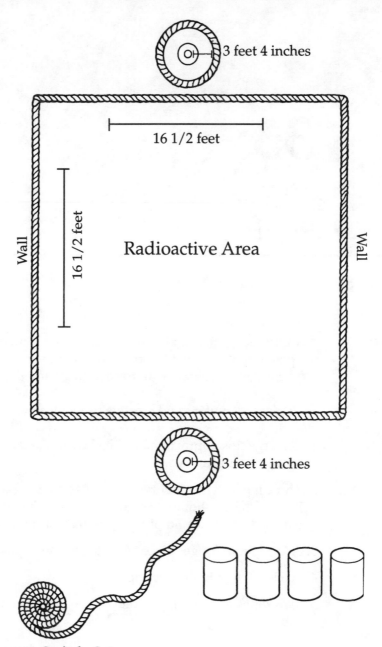

Figure 9. Switch: Setup.

6. Give the observers and the team the following instructions:

"You are in a spaceship. The robotics that usually switch the position of the two energy orbs that power your ship are inoperative due to a computer glitch. These spheres safely generate energy that is similar to both atomic and electrical energy as long as they are switched or re-polarized every 30 days. The orbs are scheduled to be switched today. You must improvise a manual way to repolarize them to avert an explosion that will destroy the ship.

"The rope square encases a radioactive area that is deadly to the touch. The two sides of the square that cross from one sphere to the other represent walls. The circles around the orbs signal the fact that humans cannot get within 3 feet of the orbs without instantly going blind or mute.

"The orbs on the tins will explode if contacted by anything other than the rope or the tins. The tins represent extra pedestals that are completely impervious to radiation. The ball on the ground is a dud which is harmless. The rope is unaffected by direct contact with the spheres. Any part of the rope that touches the radioactive area in the square, however, will become contaminated. Anyone touching that portion of the rope will immediately become blind or mute."

7. Tell the observers to watch for instances of teamwork and to tell you if anyone gets within 3 feet of an orb, or touches a contaminated section of rope or the ground in the radiated square. Anyone who dies becomes an observer. Whether a contaminated participant loses sight or voice and for how long is up to you.

8. Tell the team that calculations have indicated that in 20–35 minutes the spheres will explode. Introduce this time restraint when and if you feel it is appropriate.

9. When they have switched the balls or exploded, conduct a review.

Commentary

While simulating the switch using the extra materials is standard and predictable, crossing the radiated square allows for considerable creativity. Walking on top of the tins which are rotated across, or walking in them, are common but difficult solutions. First flattening the tins and then walking on them is an easier solution. Failure to use this approach illustrates a basic paradox related to creativity—to create is to destroy. Dealing with blindness and muteness is an individual trial that also shifts the group dynamics as those handicapped are usually highly active participants, if not leaders. Death gives rise to interesting discussions from the perspective of both the victims and the survivors. In addition to injuries and death, which raise questions about the quality of the team's effort, there is a distinct possibility that the team will fail.

Variations

1. Variations to make the exercise easier involve decreasing the distance to cross, adding tins, or reducing the consequences of contamination.

2. Variations which make this activity harder involve eliminating the extra ball, reducing the number of tins, or increasing the distance between the orbs.

34

Hog Tied

Summary   Groups of three are joined together at the ankles to form a four-legged unit. One person is in the middle with their legs joined to two outside people. The people on the outside each have a free leg. These triads then perform a series of co-operative tasks.

Objectives   To provide team building, energizing, and problem solving.

Materials   1. Two 3–foot lengths of soft 1/2–3/4 inch rope for each triad.

2. Sections of a bicycle inner tube or towelling can be substituted. A soccer-, volley-, or similar-sized ball that is a little under-inflated.

Time Limit   15–30 minutes.

Procedure   1. Team size is 8–17 with larger groups forming multiple teams. Tell the group to divide into groups of three.

2. Give each triad two ropes. Give one rope to the single person or the two participants who are left over.

3. Explain that the groups of three are to join together at the ankles to form a four-legged unit. One person is in the middle with his/her legs joined to two outside people. The people on the outside each have a free leg. Explain that they can move in whatever manner they choose.

4. Note that dyads similarly join legs to form a three-legged unit but can only travel on their outside legs. A single person must join his/her own ankles together and can only move by hopping.

5. Participants' first task is to form a circle.

6. Once they have formed a circle, ask participants to cross over to the other side of the circle without bumping into anyone. Note that if they bump into someone they must rotate three times saying "Excuse us! Excuse us! Excuse us!" Then those bumped must also rotate three times while responding with an even more demonstrative "It's all right!, it's all right! it's all right!"

7. When participants have crossed to the other side, ask them to seat themselves carefully in the circle.

8. When all are seated, tell participants their last task will be to pass the ball around the circle using only their outstretched legs. When the group is satisfied with their performance with the ball ask them to stand up carefully and untie their legs.

9. Conduct a review.

Commentary

This is an energizing activity that mirrors the way many teams operate while actually on the job. Thus it can raise relevant issues about coordination, both within and between small subgroups.

Variation

A comparison of the emotions that are related to co-operation and competition can be generated by beginning the activity with a race.

35

Lean on Me

Summary   The group works in pairs to do exercises that involve physical support and trust to accomplish. They then alternate partners to allow many, if not all, possible dyads to work together.

Objectives   To explore team building, trust, and communication.

Materials   None.

Time Limit   20 minutes or longer depending on the size of the group and how many different pairings you allow. It would take seven pairings and 35–45 minutes for every member of a group of eight to pair up with every other member; nine pairings and 40–55 minutes for all pairings of a group of ten, etc.

Procedure   1. Note that parts of this activity may be inadvisable for those with back problems. Ask participants to screen themselves. Explain that they will need to communicate clearly during each of the exercises that follow to ensure safety. Divide the group into pairs who know each other well. Explain that there will be several different pairings. If there is an uneven number, note that the extra person will pair up with someone next time and that a different person should be unpaired with each new pairing.

2. Instruct each dyad to stand back to back with their elbows interlocked. When they are all in position, tell them to decide which of the pair will go first. Note that they will take turns doing the next activity.

3. Tell participants that the lead person should bend over gradually until the other person is off the ground and then lower them back down and switch roles. Ask a pair to demonstrate or do so yourself with the extra person. Then ask all the dyads to do it.

4. Tell participants to remain back to back with their elbows locked while gradually lowering themselves to a sitting position and then, when they are ready, to return to their standing position. Ask a pair to demonstrate or do so yourself with the extra person. Then ask all the dyads to do it.

5. Next, ask participants to stand facing each other about 3 feet apart. Tell them to lean into each other and clasp each others' thumbs rather than interlocking their fingers. Their goal is to see how far apart they can get by

leaning into and supporting each other while gradually moving their feet farther and farther back. Demonstrate with the extra person or ask a pair to do so. Then tell all the participants to do it.

6. Next, ask participants to face each other again about 3 feet apart. Tell them to fall toward each other using their open palms to break their fall. Then they must push themselves back to their original standing position without stumbling. Their goal is to be as far apart as possible. Ask a pair to demonstrate or do so yourself with the extra person. Then ask all the participants to do it.

7. When they have finished and if time dictates, tell participants to switch partners and repeat the sequence of back bends, back-to-back, and forward leans. They should continue to switch partners until all have paired up or your time runs out.

8. Conduct a review.

Commentary This is a good activity to use early in a program to engage a group in discussions of trust and risk taking. It works well as a lead-in to **Quality Circles**, the next activity.

Variation Eliminate the back bend to save time.

36

Quality Circles

Summary
: A team of 7–12 forms a circle to conduct a series of co-operative activities which are then assessed for quality of performance and/or outcome.

Objectives
: To explore team building, energizing, and quality assessment.

Materials
: 1. A volleyball.

    2. A length of soft 3/4–1 inch rope. Tie the ends of the rope together to form a circle with a circumference long enough to allow the full team to sit around it. Use a knot with back-up knots that you are confident will not slip.

    3. One large balloon for each participant, plus a few extras in case of accidents.

Time Limit
: 30–45 minutes.

Procedure
: 1. Tell the group that it will conduct a series of co-operative activities and after each activity will assess it for quality of performance and/or outcome.

    2. Ask participants the following questions: How will you know whether you have performed well as a team? produced a good outcome? Can you perform well and have a mediocre outcome and vice versa?

    3. When participants are clear about the distinction between intra-team performance and the product of that interaction, place the joined rope on the ground in a circle. Ask the group to sit around the outside of the rope. Their task is to bring themselves to a stand by pulling on the rope. When they are up, their next task is to lower themselves back down again. Tell them to begin.

    4. When they have finished, ask participants to discuss the quality of their product based on how smoothly and simultaneously they moved up and down. Note that the quality of their team performance is a measure of the degree to which everyone feels their ideas were welcomed and listened to, personal safety was considered, and no one's feelings, toes, hands, or anything else were hurt.

    5. Next, ask participants to sit in a circle with their arms extended straight out toward the center and their hands clenched in a fist. Their task is to transport the ball around the circle as smoothly and quickly as they can using only their arms.

6. When they have finished, ask participants to discuss the quality of their product based on speed and smoothness and their interpersonal process.

7. Next, give each participant a balloon and tell them to blow it up to near-full capacity and tie it off. Demonstrate in order to avoid tiny balloons or explosions.

8. When the balloons are ready tell the pairs that one of them should hold their balloon in front of them while the other presses theirs on the back of the person in front. Hands cannot be used and must be flapped as though they were wings. Their goal is to link up with the others in a line so that everyone but the front person will be holding their balloon by pressing it against someone else's back.

9. When participants have completed the task tell them their next goal is to form a circle, holding the balloons in the same way. Once the circle is formed, have a discussion on the quality of their product and performance.

Commentary

This activity is an effective means of introducing ways to think about and assess teamwork. It can also be used to make the distinction between task-related and group maintenance behaviour. This activity is an effective lead-in to **Co-operative Circles**, the next activity, which looks at how subgroups interact with each other to attain a common goal.

Variations

1. Activities can be omitted.

2. The activity can be used primarily as an energizer or to focus on other aspects of teamwork.

3. An inflatable beach ball is easier to maneuver around the circle than a volley ball.

4. The circle can attempt to pop the balloons by squeezing together.

37

Co-operative Circles

Summary	A set of exercises in which small groups of 3–5 first work alone and then need to co-operate to accomplish a common goal.
Objectives	To explore teamwork, especially as it relates to subgroups who collaborate together as a team.
Materials	A large inflatable beach ball for each subgroup.
Time Limit	40–60 minutes.
Procedure	1. Divide the team into subgroups of three or four as follows: a team of seven into a subgroup of three and one of four; eight into two groups of four; nine into three groups of three; ten into two groups of three and one group of four; eleven into two groups of four and one of three, and twelve into three groups of four.

2. Tell each subgroup to sit closely on the ground facing each other with their knees bent and the soles of their feet touching the ground. Their task is to pull each other up and then lower themselves down again. Be ready to break any falls.

3. Next, tell participants their goal is to repeat the same process but this time their aim is to get as many of them standing as they can.

4. When they have completed the task to their satisfaction, ask participants to compare the experiences in terms of the advantages and disadvantages of working with the smaller and larger teams.

5. Next, tell participants to return to their original small groups. Give each subgroup a ball and tell them their task is to create a web by joining hands to arms or wrists in such a way that each person has a hold on at least one other person. This web will then be used to keep the beach ball off the ground by bumping it into the air. Participants should set a goal for so many bumps and try to reach it. Note that they will have only 4–6 minutes and signal the start of the activity.

6. When the time is up, tell participants that in their next activity they have to work together to keep one ball off the ground for as many bumps as they

can. In this version no subgroup may hit the ball two consecutive times. Tell them they must set a goal and meet it. There is no time limit. Depending on your time constraints you can ask participants to lower their goal if they are having problems or raise it if they achieve it easily.

7. When they have completed the task ask participants to compare their experiences in terms of the advantages and disadvantages of working with the smaller and larger teams.

Commentary　This set of activities promotes awareness and consultation about working in larger and smaller groups and the issues involved in teams that often work as smaller subsets of the larger body.

Variations　1. You can omit an activity as either can stand alone.

2. The emphasis can be on interteam issues as well as intrateam issues.

38

Co-operative Machines

Summary Groups of 3–4 form a series of machines through the creative use of their minds and bodies.

Objectives To explore teamwork, planning versus implementation, and the blocks to and facilitation of team creativity.

Materials None.

Time Limit 50–75 minutes.

Procedure

1. Divide the team into subgroups of three or four as follows: a team of seven into a subgroup of three and one of four; eight into two groups of four; nine into three groups of three; ten into two groups of three and one group of four; eleven into two groups of four and one of three; and twelve into three groups of four.

2. Tell participants they have 15 minutes to prepare to demonstrate the following machines: a typewriter, a ski-lift, an old-fashioned egg-beater, a bicycle, a copying machine, a juicer, a Ferris wheel, and a toaster.

3. When they are ready or the time is up, have the teams take turns depicting each machine. Rotate the order of presentation so that the team that initially goes first goes last the next time, and so on.

4. When the presentations are complete, ask participants to compare what they had to do and how they felt while planning as opposed to performing.

5. Next, ask the whole group to decide on two machines to present. Everyone must be a part of both machines. One machine should be selected from those that have already been given and one should be an original. Give participants 15 minutes after which they must perform.

6. When participants have performed, have a discussion on planning as opposed to implementation and the factors that facilitate and block team creativity.

Commentary   This activity works best with a group that has already spent time in more structured exercises. It helps team members to appreciate the roles of planning and implementation while becoming aware of their preference for one or the other as an aspect of teamwork. The activity can also help a team to develop norms and/or procedures that will foster creativity and/or remove barriers to creativity. This activity can be used effectively in conjunction with **Co-operative Circles** (game 37) and/or **Values in Action** (game 41).

Variations   1. The activity can be used as a quick energizer by giving each group one machine at a time and asking for a performance in a minute. This approach can be used alone or compared with the original in terms of the role of time constraints that sometimes help and sometimes hinder creativity.

2. A longer version involves more performances by the full team.

39

Team Awareness

Summary   Two activities demonstrate how a team can rapidly attend to and communicate with its members without speaking.

Objectives   To explore teamwork, team awareness, and silent communication.

Materials   None.

Time Limit   20–30 minutes.

Procedure

1. Divide the team into subgroups of three or four as follows: a team of seven into a subgroup of three and one of four; eight into two groups of four; nine into three groups of three; ten into two groups of three and one group of four; eleven into two groups of four and one of three; and twelve into three groups of four.

2. Tell participants that in this exercise they each hold a clenched fist in front of them and shake it while chanting in unison "Apples! Oranges! Bananas!" On "Bananas" each must display any number of fingers from none to five. Their goal is for a group of three to display 11 fingers or a group of four to show 13 fingers without speaking to each other.

3. When they have finished, tell the whole group to do the same task as a team. The ratio or group size to number of fingers is as follows: 7 to 23; 8 to 25; 9 to 29; 10 to 31; 11 to 35; and 12 to 37; etc.

4. When participants have completed the task to their satisfaction ask them to explain how they were able to achieve their goal.

5. Next, ask participants to stand in a U-shaped line and tell them that they may not speak until they complete their next task. Tell them that in this task they may raise both their arms and flap them whenever they wish as long as they continue to do so for 5 seconds. Their goal is to flap so that the specified numbers of group members, no more and no less, are flapping for at least a minute. The requisite number of flappers is as follows: three for a team of 7–10, four for a team of 11–20 and five for a group of 20 or more. Ask for a volunteer(s) to time them.

113

6. Remind participants that they may not speak until they have succeeded in keeping their exact number flapping for a minute, then begin.

7. When participants have succeeded, ask them to explain how they were able to achieve their goal. Then ask them if there are any analogies between what they did in the activity and what they can do in teamwork situations on the job to ensure that such awareness is present.

Commentary

This is an excellent activity for discussing how awareness of non-verbal team communication needs to be made explicit and verbal when it signals the potential sidestepping of the achievement of such matters as full and frank team discussion or in-depth and comprehensive team understanding.

Variations

1. Either of these activities can stand alone.

2. The fingers activity can be used to further the subgroup, full-team comparison activities in **Co-operative Circles** (game 37).

40

Globe-trotters

Summary   A humorous and energizing three-event relay race between two or more teams involving air, water balloons, and grapefruit.

Objectives   To explore teamwork, planning, creativity, multiple goals, competition, and energizing.

Materials

1. One small grapefruit, one large balloon, and one water balloon for each relay team. Have extra-large balloons and water balloons. Test the grapefruits to see how difficult they are to carry and pass under the chin. Err on the side of smaller grapefruits and select those of similar size.

2. A bucket of water to store the water balloons. (If it is a hot day the balloons will spontaneously explode if left out in the sun.)

3. Two boundary ropes 10 feet long to indicate the starting and finishing lines.

Time Limit   30–45 minutes or less if fewer events are used.

Procedure

1. Place the boundary ropes about 26–30 feet apart and put the bucket of water balloons 3 feet beyond the finishing line.

2. Explain that the next activity will be a relay race. If the group has an odd number of participants, ask for a volunteer referee. Otherwise, be the referee yourself. The referee will observe teams during the planning stage, call fouls, and call the winner in the event of a close finish in any of the legs.

3. Divide the group into two or more even-numbered teams of four or more.

4. Place the teams behind the starting line with a deflated balloon, a slightly under-filled water balloon, and a grapefruit and tell them that the relay will begin in 10–15 minutes.

5. Instruct participants as follows:

   "There are three legs to the relay race. You will pair up for the first leg. At the Go signal inflate the balloon. The first pair places the balloon between their faces and, with their hands behind their backs, walks across to the opposite line and returns. Once across the starting line, transfer the balloon to the next pair, without either pair using their hands. If a balloon gets away from a pair, it may be picked up only after it has hit the ground. When the last pair returns to the start, begin the second lap.

"The second lap is run individually and again no hands may be used except at the start. The first player must tuck the grapefruit under his/her chin and cross to the opposite boundary and back. The grapefruit is then placed under the next player's chin, and so on until the last one returns to the start. The last person must then pass the grapefruit to the next-to-last person, and so on until the first runner has it. This ends the second lap. Anyone who drops the grapefruit while carrying it must begin again by hopping on one leg back to behind the starting line. If the grapefruit is dropped while being passed, the two people involved must hop on one foot while singing a chorus of London Bridge is falling down before attempting to pass the grapefruit again. Hands may not be used to carry or pass the grapefruit— they may only be used to pick up drops.

"The last lap starts with the team lining up single file with the first person immediately behind the starting line and holding the water balloon. The lead person passes the balloon overhead to the person behind who does likewise until the last person receives it. That person then runs to the front of the line and passes the balloon under his/her legs to the person behind and so forth until the last person receives it and runs to the front and passes it overhead. This alternating over-and-under passing procedure continues until the original lead person is again at the front of the line and the relay race is over.

"Should a balloon burst, the person who burst it must hop to get a new one from the bucket behind the opposite line.

"The ways to win the race are as follows: (a) win the first balloon leg; (b) be the first team to complete the grapefruit leg; (c) win the overall relay race by being the first to finish the water balloon leg; (d) being the team with fewest errors based on the total number of balloon drops plus grapefruit drops plus water balloon bursts.

"Each team should assign a member to track its errors. Participants are on their honor in counting errors."

6. When the time is up or all the teams are ready, signal the start of the relay race.

7. When the race is over announce the winners and discuss the exercise.

Commentary

This is a hilarious race that takes thought, planning, and practice or piloting rather than speed to win. Running is rare, as even the grapefruit relay must be carried out cautiously. Planning and creativity range from how much to inflate the balloons and pairing up with those of similar height to developing techniques for passing balloons and grapefruits. The multiple goals and competitive aspects of the exercise can open up some involved discussions about how those issues are played out in the work environment. A camera is a must for this activity.

Variations

1. This exercise can work using any one or two of the relays.

2. Under-inflated water balloons will rarely break, while over-inflated ones burst easily.

41

Values in Action

Summary A team is asked to suggest four values. They translate each of these values first into a movement and then into a four-movement sequence, which is accompanied by their humming of the melody of their choice.

Objectives To explore goal and value setting, creativity, and team building.

Materials None.

Time Limit 45–70 minutes.

Procedure
1. Select a private setting. Decide whether or not you want to do this activity at a location that is in or near to woods. If woods are available you can allow the team to use the natural materials available. Nothing is to be pulled up or cut down.

2. Tell the team that their first task is to suggest four values. The values must be stated in one word or a short phrase that can serve as a guide for their interactions or how they want to deal with each other. Give them 15–20 minutes.

3. When the time is up or the task is done, they have 15–20 minutes to translate each of these values first into a movement and finally into a dance using all four movements in sequence. They must also accompany themselves by humming a melody of their choice. They must all take part in planning and presenting the values.

4. When the participants are ready, ask them to perform the dance.

5. Conduct a review.

Commentary This is an effective activity for the earlier stages of team building with all the members of an intact team. It emphasizes the importance of translating values into action not only in the dance that they create but also in their future interactions together. Encourage their use of the movements as a shorthand way to remind each other to put their values into practice when they fail to do so.

This activity works well in conjunction with **Co-operative Machines** (game 38).

Variations

1. The values may also be goals for the way in which their products or services are perceived.

2. If you are working with two or more intact teams, have the performances held indoors accompanied by the recorded music of their choice.

42

Over, Under, and Through

Summary
Two teams are captured by a highly evolved alien race who has set up a test involving going over, under, and through a radiation barrier to determine whether or not one or both teams will go free. The alien race will free a team only if it behaves in its own best interest. The circumstances of the task make offering help to, and soliciting aid from, the other team an advantageous strategy from a logical and practical perspective. Culturally conditioned competitiveness will keep the teams from working together.

Objectives
To explore co-operation versus competition, teamwork within and between teams, quality, ethics, and evaluation.

Materials
A large ball of thick string or thin nylon cord.

Time Limit
50–80 minutes.

Procedure
1. Find a private area with four trees that roughly form a rectangle with two opposing sides 10–12 feet apart and at least 6 feet 6 inches wide. The shape need not have right-angles or parallel sides, but it needs to be large enough to contain both teams without crowding. The ground between and around the trees should be relatively level and free from rocks, roots, bushes, or any other obstructions to safe footing. There should be no branches lower than 6 feet 6 inches from the ground.

2. Run the string tautly around the four trees at the following approximate heights: 12 inches, 30 inches, and 50 inches.

3. Criss-cross the string between the two 10–12 foot sides so that no one can fit through any of the openings between the string.

4. Make a window 20–22 inches wide in the middle of each of the 6 foot 6 inches (or larger) sides by running two pieces of string perpendicular to and between the top (50-inch high) string and the middle (30-inch high) string.

5. Criss-cross string on the outside of each window so that the windows are the only spaces between the top and middle strings through which a person could fit. Figure 10 illustrates the window and the lower space that participants can pass through, the bottom space which they can crawl under, and the top line which they can be passed over.

119

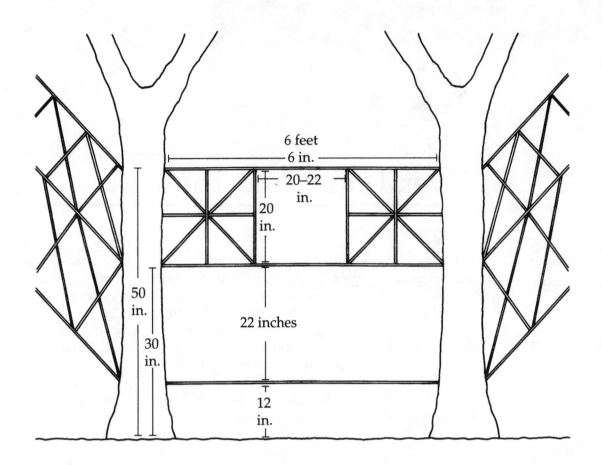

Figure 10. Over, Under, and Through: Setup (the identical rear windows are not depicted).

6. Bring the group to the rectangle of trees. Briefly describe the activity and ask for one and preferably two or three volunteers to be the alien observers.

7. Divide the remainder of the group into two approximately equal teams of 7–12 members each. Omit the observers if a team would otherwise be smaller than seven.

8. Place the teams on opposite sides of the rectangle so that they are looking at each other through the windowed sides.

9. Tell participants they are two teams of space travelers who were captured by a highly evolved alien race. These aliens have set up the following test to determine whether or not one or both will go free:

"You are on opposite sides of two radiation barriers. Your goal is to change places. You must cross through the common area between the two barriers to accomplish the switch. You may not go around the barriers. You may go over, under, and through the barriers based on the following constraints that apply equally to both barriers:

- Only one person may crawl under the lowest space and only two may pass through the middle level.

- There is no limit on how many may go through the upper window or over the top.

- There must be at least three people on either side for someone to be passed over the top.

- No one may dive or be thrown through the barrier.

- If anyone touches the corded barrier while passing through it, they must return.

- Anyone touching the corded barrier or entering a space that has already reached its limit suffers from radiation. The progression of effects from radioactive contact is the loss of speech on the first contact, loss of sight on the second contact, paralysis of arms and legs on the third, and death on the fourth. Loss of speech, sight, and the use of limbs lasts for 5 minutes.

- Death is permanent.

Each team must monitor itself regarding touches and enforcing the 5-minute handicaps. You are on your honor."

10. Tell participants they have 20–40 minutes to accomplish the switch. Smaller groups take less time and time pressure makes a co-operative solution more compelling.

11. Take the alien observers aside and tell them that the task can be carried out by each team independently of the other. Explain that if the two teams assist each other by lifting each other in the common area and/or leaving one of the two lower areas open for each other, the task becomes much easier for both. Tell them they must decide which, if any, team goes free based first on the degree to which it behaves in its own best interest by offering help to and soliciting aid from the other team and, second, on the degree to which it keeps high standards by calling touches and enforcing handicaps. You can delete, add to, or amend these criteria as your learning objectives dictate.

12. When the time is up or when participants have completed the switch, give the alien observers 5 minutes to prepare before sharing their verdicts on which, if any, teams will go free and why.

Also inform participants that you and they must be ready to break the fall of those being passed through the upper window and over the top. Note the need to have someone inside the rectangle and that priority must be given to protecting those being passed over the top.

13. Conduct a review.

Commentary

This exercise can astonish groups with the fact that teams tend to work independently of, if not competitively against, each other even though their collaboration is beneficial to both. Few groups collaborate when this exercise is used early in a program. Use it late in a program to demonstrate or test for the development of intergroup teamwork. **Beach-ball Bump,** the next activity, is a good companion exercise.

Issues of quality and integrity related to calling touches are easily brought out in this activity. It also provides an excellent example of the difficulties of not knowing what criteria are being applied to assess a team's performance.

Variations

1. Vary the size and/or number of openings. The sizes given are moderate to easy for most teams.

2. Three trees that form an 80–90 degree angle with each other can be used. The two barriers are formed between the middle tree and the two outside trees. While even closer proximity is achieved in the common area formed inside the 80–90 degree angle, teams still tend to ignore and/or compete with each other.

3. The activity can also be used with just one team using two trees.

43

Beach-ball Bump

Summary   Two teams start at opposite ends of a field and must volley a beach ball to the other side as quickly as possible without the ball ever hitting the ground.

Objectives   To explore co-operation/competition, teamwork within and between teams, energizing, and goal setting.

Materials   1. Two differently colored, large, inflatable beach balls. Leave the balls deflated and sterilize after each use.

2. Two ropes for boundary lines.

Time Limit   20–45 minutes.

Procedure   1. Locate a large athletic playing field or a similar open area with good footing.

2. Place the boundary ropes 100–200 feet apart. Leave at least 16 feet of flat, open area beyond each boundary.

3. Bring your group to the middle of the field. Describe the activity and recruit those with bad ankles, knees, etc. as observers. You will need at least two observers unless you time one of the teams.

4. Divide the remaining participants into two preferably equal teams.

5. Tell participants they will start at opposite ends of a field with a deflated beach ball. On the signal to begin they must inflate the ball and place it on the ground behind the starting line. The opening volley from the ground must be made without the use of hands. All other bumps can be made with hands, feet, heads, shoulders, and so on. The goal is to volley the beach ball to the other side as quickly as possible. If any of the following rules is violated the team must begin again from behind the starting line:

- The ball may not be hit consecutively by the same person.
- The ball must be bumped as in volleyball. No throws or carries are allowed.
- The beach ball must not touch the ground.

123

6. When everyone is clear about the instructions, give each team a deflated beach ball and at least one observer and direct them to opposite sides of the field.

7. When they are ready, signal the start.

8. When both teams have finished, ask each how long they took. When the time is given, ask, "Did you accomplish your goal?" Note that the goal is to bump the ball to the other side "as quickly as possible," not to win against the other team. They were competing with the clock, not each other. Ask if the teams hindered each other. Ask if the rules prohibited them helping each other.

9. Run the exercise again and again if there is enough energy and time.

10. Conduct a review.

Commentary

The goal is to bump the ball to the other side as quickly as possible rather than to beat the other team. The structure of the activity, however, leads to competition that often hinders performance. What frequently happens on the first try is that teams obstruct one another, which slows them both down. Co-operation between teams can improve both teams' performance. The rules do not prohibit one team hitting the other team's ball. Thus both teams can line up across the field and volley each other's beach balls across.

This exercise can lead to fruitful discussion about how to restructure work situations in order to diminish destructive competition and promote collaboration between teams. It may also highlight assumed, unwritten rules that hinder the co-operation between teams that could enhance overall performance.

Variations

1. Start the activity with two teams striving for their best possible time. Structure the activity so that the teams start independently whenever they choose. Then structure it as a race. Finally, have participants work as one team against the clock. This variation can lead to interesting observations about the differences among intrateam co-operation, interteam competition, and interteam collaboration.

2. One team can work on this activity. As a goal-setting exercise, make their first try the baseline time. Then ask them to set a target time. Participants then make repeated attempts to reach or raise their target. Additional balls can be added and/or the field can be lengthened to increase the challenge progressively. Also, add restraints such as limiting each team member to no more than two or three hits, hopping on one foot, or moving only backward.

44

Wiggle

Summary

A group forms a circle. Two large bicycle inner tubes are evenly spaced between them so that when participants all join hands each inner tube is suspended over the linked hands. The participants' task is to send the tubes around the circle and back to their original position without releasing each other's hands.

Objectives

To explore teamwork, co-operation versus competition, and energizing.

Materials

Two large bicycle inner tubes for each group of 9–12 participants. Remove the metal valve stems.

Time Limit

15–30 minutes.

Procedure

1. Ask the group to form a circle. Hand an inner tube to one partici pant.

2. Ask the group to join hands so that the inner tube hangs over the wrists or hands of two participants.

3. Tell the group that their task is to send the tube around the circle and back to its original position without releasing each other's hands.

4. When participants are clear about the task tell them to begin.

5. When the group has accomplished the task, hand another tube to someone on the opposite side of the circle from the first inner tube. When the two inner tubes are hanging from the hands or wrists of opposing sets of participants, designate one tube to be transferred clockwise and the other counter-clockwise.

6. When participants are clear about the task, tell them to begin.

7. When both tubes are back to their original places, ask who won. There is a tendency to assume that the winners are the first tube to return and/or the couple who began with that tube.

8. Note that when everyone works together on a common task the idea of winning does not really apply. Conduct a review and discussion.

Commentary   The tendency to view fundamentally co-operative endeavors competitively is illustrated through this task. The activity can lead to discussions of actual work tasks which similarly may be viewed inappropriately as competitive.

Variations
1. For an easier task, have all the tubes moving in the same direction.

2. For larger groups, hand two more tubes to two opposite pairs of participants so that when they all join hands four inner tubes are evenly spaced around the circle of linked hands. One pair of opposing tubes must travel clockwise, while the other pair travels counter-clockwise.

45

The Chicken

Summary   A warm-up stretch which simulates the movements of a chicken.

Objectives   To explore team building using an energizer or a limbering-up exercise to prepare for a more strenuous exercise such as a relay race.

Materials   None.

Time Limit   5–10 minutes.

Procedure   1. Practice this stretch in front of a mirror to be sure you can model a well-synchronized and exaggerated chicken-walk. Be sure no one catches you mid-cluck as no one will believe that you are rehearsing an athletic stretch. For the method actors and urbanites among you, a visit to a hen-house may be helpful!

2. Tell the group that the next exercise will be a stretch that you will present by demonstrating it step by step. After you have shown them a section of the stretch, they will copy it. Then you will add a second section and they will copy the two moves. This process will continue until everyone is doing the entire stretch.

3. The moves are described as follows:

   - "Repeatedly lift your knees, one after the other, as high as you can while remaining in place.

   - Bend your arms at the elbows and flap them up and down against your side as if you were trying to fly.

   - Add the jutting of your head like a chicken, forward at the neck and back to its original position.

   - Add a clucking sound, and instead of staying in place begin moving like a chicken."

4. A review and discussion are optional.

Commentary   Use with groups that have already demonstrated a moderate level of cohesion. This exercise can build group solidarity and help to break tension by creating an opportunity to behave ridiculously.

Variation   When the group has been moving about for a while, instruct them to form a single-file line behind you and then a circle. You are now ready to introduce your next exercise.

46

Team Tag

Summary Teams of three participants compete to be the first team to pin all its clothespins on opponents' backs while keeping at least one team member clothespin-free.

Objectives To explore teamwork, planning, organization, problem solving, and energizing.

Materials 1. Wooden clothespins. Each participant needs three clothespins. There are three participants to a team. Each team has its own color of clothespin. Dye the clothespins in different colors using a solution of food coloring and water. If you have four teams, you will need nine blue, nine red, nine green, and nine yellow clothespins.

2. One long or four shorter boundary ropes.

Time Limit 20–40 minutes.

Procedure 1. Use the boundary rope to frame a playing area of approximately 400 square feet.

2. Designate as observers those wearing jackets or tops which will not be easy to pin. Divide the group into teams of three.

3. Explain that this activity is a walking tag game in which team members clip their clothespins on the back of opposing team members' shirts or jackets.

4. Present the rules as follows:

   • "You cannot remove a clothespin from yourself.

   • You may pick up one of your team's clothespins if it is on the ground.

   • You may walk quickly but not jog or run.

   • You must stay within the boundaries at all times."

5. Note that the observers can disqualify any team whom they feel has violated the rules.

6. Tell participants that the winner is the first team to rid itself of all its clothespins so that none of them are on the ground and at least one team member has no clothespins on his/her back.

7. Quickly begin the game after you have given the members of each team three similarly colored clothespins. You do not want them to have time to plan a strategy.

8. If there is a winner or if a winner has not emerged after about 5 minutes, call a time out. At this stage allow each team a few minutes to plan.

9. When the planning time is up, start the game. If no winner emerges after about 5 minutes end the game and declare them all winners.

10. Conduct a review.

Commentary

Winning in this activity is infrequent and more often occurs in the unplanned segment. The unplanned and planned segments of this activity dramatically illustrate the role and function of planning and organization. The activity is also complex enough to provoke a variety of different problem-solving strategies.

Variation

For groups of more than 15, use teams of four and an area of approximately 550 square feet. Using two clothespins per player makes a winner more likely, while using four makes it extremely unlikely that any team will win.

47

Wet Dog Wiggle

Summary   A warm-up activity in which participants mimic a wet dog shaking itself after coming out of the water.

Objectives   To practice a warm-up and energizer.

Materials   None.

Time Limit   5–10 minutes.

Procedure   1. Practice this stretch in front of a mirror to be sure you can model a well-synchronized and exaggerated wet dog wiggle. Should someone see you rehearsing, tell them it is an esoteric yoga stretch. A visit to the beach on a warm day guarantees at least one real-life exhibition of the wet dog wiggle.

2. Tell the group that the next exercise will be a warm-up that you will present by demonstrating it progressively stage by stage. When you have shown participants a section, they will repeat it. Then you will add a second section and they will copy the two moves. This process will continue until everyone is doing the entire movement.

3. Describe the moves as follows

   • "Begin by setting your feet a little more than shoulders width apart with your knees bent slightly in an athletic stance.

   • Start to jiggle or shake your legs so that your knees are pointing in toward each other and back out again. The motion is small and vibratory rather than large and swinging.

   • Next add the twisting of your hips and upper torso in opposite directions so that when your left shoulder is jutting out to the left, your right hip is sticking out to the right and vice versa. This movement is a rapid and exaggerated version of the dance 'The Twist.'

   • Now bend your arms at the elbow and flail them around leaving your wrists loose so that your hands flap around.

   • Finally add the twirling and shaking of your head."

4. Review and discussion are optional.

Commentary   Use this activity with groups who have already demonstrated a moderate level of cohesion. This exercise can build group solidarity and help break tension by creating an opportunity for looking and acting ridiculously.

Variation   Ask the group to continue the wiggle while forming a single-file line behind you and then to form a circle. You are now ready to introduce your next exercise.

48

Flight

Summary	Teams are given paper and paper clips. Their goal is to create the largest number of airplanes that travel beyond a designated point.
Objectives	To explore teamwork and creative problem solving.
Materials	1. Ten sheets of paper and ten paper clips for each participant. The sheets of paper should all be the same size. Previously copied or other used paper is fine. 2. One sheet of the same paper and one paper clip for yourself. 3. A starting line rope.
Time Limit	30–40 minutes.
Procedure	1. Divide the group into teams of three or four depending on the number of participants. 2. Give each member of each team ten sheets of paper and ten paperclips. 3. Tell participants their task is to create paper airplanes using just one paper clip and one piece of paper for each plane. Their goal is to arrive at a design that will produce airplanes that travel farther than any of the other teams' planes. 4. Tell participants that they have 15 minutes to produce the planes. They should be made in secret so that no one can duplicate anyone else's design. When the planning and production time is up, each team will submit one plane. Then the teams will line up behind the starting line. Each participant must launch nine or ten planes when the signal is given. 5. Take questions and tell participants the 15-minute time allowance has begun. 6. When the time is up call the teams back together. Take their samples and note which plane belongs to which team. Tell them that only those planes that were completed prior to the signal that the production period had ended may be flown.

7. Instruct participants to line up by team and prepare to launch all their planes on your signal. Give the signal.

8. Tell the group that all the planes that travel farther than yours will be counted to determine the winner. This should be the first time you reveal your method of determining which planes flew the farthest. Then take your paper clip, crumple your paper around it into a tight ball, and throw it as far as you can.

9. Determine if there is a winner and discuss the exercise.

Commentary

This activity demonstrates how descriptive sets about how things are supposed to look limit creativity. It can lead into a more involved discussion of functional sets (for example, a hammer is only used to pound or pull nails) and other blocks to creativity and improvisation. The activity is a good companion activity to **Ringer,** the next activity. Make sure there is a wide interval between the times in which you use them.

Variations

1. If it is windy you may want to do this activity in a large indoor area.

2. You can give participants more planning time and tell them that each team member will launch just one plane. This leads to experimentation that increases the likelihood that someone will come up with the ball shape.

49

Ringer

Summary	Two or more teams compete to score the most points at a game of ring toss.
Objectives	To explore teamwork and creative problem solving.
Materials	1. Each team needs four ring-toss stands and six rings. The stands should have a single post as a target. You can substitute a stake driven in the ground for three of the four stands. This substitution reduces the number of ring-toss sets you will need to purchase at the toyshop.
	2. Enough powdered lime to make a 3–foot boundary line for each team.
	3. A boundary rope 10–13 feet long.
	4. A pocket calculator.
Time Limit	35-50 minutes.
Procedure	1. Find a location for setting up the competition that will afford the teams easy access to private places in which they can practice and discuss. Create a 3- foot boundary line with powdered lime. This is the toss line. Place a ring-toss stand 3 feet away from the toss line. Now take six rings in your hand and, keeping your toes from touching or crossing the toss line, lie down on your belly beside the stand. With your free hand place the stand in front of you at the farthest distance that still allows you to place all six rings over its post easily.
	2. Measure the distance from the toss line to the stand's post and place the next stand a similar distance from the first one. The distance is usually from 6 1/2–8 feet. The third stand is placed the same distance from the second. Repeat this set up (a toss line and three evenly spaced stands) at 3 foot intervals for each additional team. Then place the boundary rope 3 feet behind the toss line. This is the viewing line. The set up for three teams should resemble Figure 11.

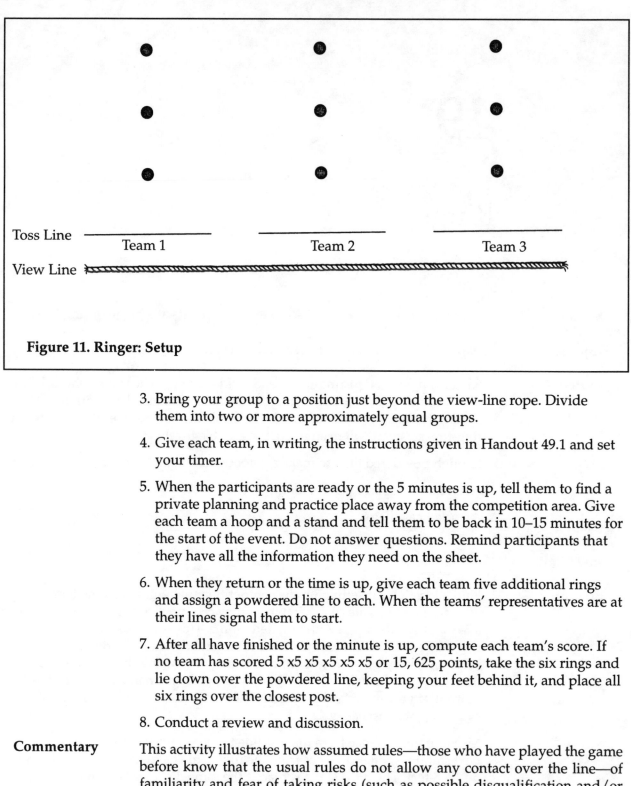

Toss Line ——————————— ——————————— ———————————
             Team 1   Team 2   Team 3

View Line

Figure 11. Ringer: Setup

3. Bring your group to a position just beyond the view-line rope. Divide them into two or more approximately equal groups.

4. Give each team, in writing, the instructions given in Handout 49.1 and set your timer.

5. When the participants are ready or the 5 minutes is up, tell them to find a private planning and practice place away from the competition area. Give each team a hoop and a stand and tell them to be back in 10–15 minutes for the start of the event. Do not answer questions. Remind participants that they have all the information they need on the sheet.

6. When they return or the time is up, give each team five additional rings and assign a powdered line to each. When the teams' representatives are at their lines signal them to start.

7. After all have finished or the minute is up, compute each team's score. If no team has scored 5 x5 x5 x5 x5 x5 or 15, 625 points, take the six rings and lie down over the powdered line, keeping your feet behind it, and place all six rings over the closest post.

8. Conduct a review and discussion.

Commentary   This activity illustrates how assumed rules—those who have played the game before know that the usual rules do not allow any contact over the line—of familiarity and fear of taking risks (such as possible disqualification and/or inability to reach the post) can be barriers to creative problem solving. The activity can lead into a more involved discussion of functional sets (for example, a knife is only used to cut) and other blocks to creativity and improvisation. This activity is a good companion to **Flight** (game 48) and/or **Nuclear Reactor I** (game 56). Use a wide time interval between them.

Variations

1. Elimination of the view-line restriction allows participants to experiment with reaching over. You can add "While powdered lime on a team member's foot or shoe is evidence of a foul, you are on your honor" to rule 3 of their instructions (see Handout 49.1). While "steps" are by definition made with a foot, this option makes the restriction more explicit and thus may lead to greater confidence in using the lying-down solution.

2. You can make rope hoops that are twice as large as your originals and offer the choice of which to use with the understanding that the score with the large hoops will be divided by 2. This approach offers a linear solution to the problem (use larger hoops) which makes it less likely that a risky, lateral solution (break the assumed rules) will be sought. Even four large hoops on the middle post garners only 10 x 10 x 10 x 10 ÷ 2 or 5, 000 points.

Instructions

This activity is a team competition. In 5 minutes you will receive a ring and a stand and be asked to find a private spot out of the general vicinity of the setup in front of you. The rope is a view line that you may not pass until the actual competition.

Your task will be to get your six hoops around the three posts in front of the powdered line. Your goal will be to win the competition by scoring the most points based on the following scoring system:

1. You get five points for getting one ring on the first or closest post, ten points for one ring on the middle post, and 20 points for one ring on the farthest post. A hoop that is leaning against a post scores no points.

2. Each additional ringer multiplies your score by the original score. For example, two rings on the closest post scores 5 x 5 or 25 points, while three on the furthest post scores 20 x 20 x 20 or 8,000 points.

3. The highest team score will not constitute a win if it is not greater than 125 points or the score that the facilitator achieves based on one try, whichever is higher.

The rules are as follows:

1. Each team or its representatives will begin at the same time from behind the powdered line and will have one minute to finish.

2. Each team will have six rings.

3. If any member of a team steps on or over the powdered line, that team is automatically disqualified.

    You have all the information you need to compete.

Good luck.

Reproduced from *CHANGING PACE Outdoor Games for Experiential Learning* by Carmine M. Consalvo, HRD Press, 1996

50

Blind and Mute Carry

Summary Two blind participants carry a mute person from one point to another. All participants take turns at being blind, mute, or checking for safety.

Objectives To explore team building, communication, and trust.

Materials More than enough large, clean bandannas, of a variety of colors and designs, for each of the participants. Fold the bandannas diagonally to facilitate their use as blindfolds.

Time Limit 35–60 minutes depending on the size of the group.

Procedure 1. Find a mixed area of woods and open ground which has some boulders and/or other obstacles to go over and under. Plan a course for the group to follow.

2. Explain to the group that they will be experiencing an activity called "Blind and Mute Carry" which is designed to help them experience and examine the concepts of trust, communication, and the relationship between these two concepts in teamwork.

3. Pass around the bandannas and ask each participant to take one. Explain that the blindfolds are optional accessories and note that no one will be made fun of or in any way deliberately tricked or embarrassed while blindfolded. Peeking is a matter of challenge by choice. If participants do peek, they should do so in an inconspicuous manner that will not make the accomplishment of the team's task easier. They are on their honor.

4. Divide the group into teams of four. Tell the group that there will be three roles for each team and everyone will have a chance to experience each. Explain that each team will have two blind members. Ask for two volunteers from each team to put on their blindfolds.

5. Next ask for one volunteer from each team to be mute. Note that from now on they may not speak.

6. Note that the remaining person is a protective observer who must ensure that the other three do not have a mishap. They must intervene to keep the others from falling. When they yell "Freeze!" it is a command to stop the action for safety reasons.

7. Now tell each team that the mute person cannot walk. The teams' task will be to follow you and go exactly where you go. Give them 5 minutes to work out a system of communication and be ready to move.

8. At the end of the five minutes note the time and begin to walk. Every three to four minutes yell "Freeze!" and tell participants to change roles with one blind person becoming the protector, the other blind person becoming mute and the protector and the mute person becoming blind.

9. Give participants 3 minutes to reorganize and then continue walking for another 3–4 minutes before calling "Freeze!". Again, tell participants to change roles, to allow new people to experience being mute and the protector.

10. Repeat this process twice more, and then do a review. It is all right if someone opts not to assume certain roles.

Commentary

This activity produces considerable discussion about the importance of building good communication signals. People become aware of their preference for, or greater need for, visual or verbal information. It also opens up an appreciation for differences which people have regarding what is and is not risky. Trusting others to protect them is easier for some than trusting themselves to protect others.

Variation

1. Providing obstacles is the main way to vary this activity.

2. Participants could cross a creek or other stretch of shallow water as long as it has good footing.

You can be more challenging with this activity if the group has already done **Blind Faith** (game 3).

51

Space Squirrels

Summary   A team of space travelers must move over a dried-out riverbed on an alien planet. To cross the riverbed they must roll planks on the only things that are impervious to the riverbed's penetrating and corrosive properties—salami sausages. Unfortunately, the squirrel-like creatures that live in the riverbed ravenously gobble up the salami sausages.

Objectives   To explore team building, teamwork, and planning.

Materials   1. Three sturdy 2x10 inch planks, one 3- foot plank, one 4- foot plank, and one 6 feet long.

2. Nine logs approximately 18 inches long. They should all be of similar diameter, which can range from 2–4 inches. The length of the log should be smaller than, yet still able to hold, the width of two planks. For example, a 16-inch log could balance two planks 10 inches wide.

3. Two 13 feet or longer boundary ropes.

4. Enough powdered lime to dust lightly the area between the boundary ropes.

Time Limit   40–60 minutes.

Procedure   1. Locate a private athletic field or similar open, grassy area and place the boundary markers between 50 and 80 feet apart. The greater the distance the more time the activity will take. Difficulty is related to distance but is primarily a function of how quickly you decide the squirrels will eat the salami sausages.

2. Sprinkle the lime throughout the roped-in area.

3. Place the three boards and the nine sausages next to one of the boundary ropes outside the limed area.

4. Gather a team of 8–12 near the boards (if the group is larger use observers) and give them the following information:

"You are a team of space travelers on the New Deli planet. You must cross the dried-out riverbed in front of you to get to caves in the mountains. These caves offer you shelter from the devastating storm that is heading toward you. Based on your research of New Deli, you know that the only items you have that are impervious to the riverbed's penetrating and corrosive properties are nine salami sausages. Unfortunately the squirrel-like creatures who live in the riverbed are carnivores. They are likely to steal the salami sausages and take them to their holes to eat. They can wrench the sausages from your hands or any other unsecured situation within the riverbed area.

"The only things available to you from the environment are the three boards that will disintegrate if they touch the riverbed. If you even just briefly contact the riverbed you will lose your sight and/or speech. Contact for more than 4 seconds is deadly. The loss of one or more of your team would nullify your ability to navigate your spacecraft safely out of New Deli's orbit."

5. Tell the participants they are on their honor regarding touches and that the deadly storm will arrive in 20-30 minutes.

6. The task is most elegantly accomplished using the two longest planks and three sausages to transport the whole group at one time. The only sausages that cannot be stolen and eaten are those that are under a plank that has at least one person on it. Declare sausages as stolen and gobbled up at a pace and at intervals that you think will prompt changes in inefficient/ ineffective approaches and/or challenge teams that are working well together. In general, participants should be down to just three sausages somewhere between a half and two-thirds of the way across. Anyone who initially touches the riverbed should lose sight or speech for 2–3 minutes. Subsequent touches result in the loss of both senses for 2–3 minutes.

7. When participants have crossed the riverbed or time runs out, conduct a review and discussion.

Commentary

The activity is a good one to either test or reward a group that has begun to plan and work together well as a team or to demonstrate the need for doing so in groups that are just beginning to build a sense of being a team.

This activity often brings out sexism in which the males do all the lifting and leading. Some women apparently collude in this process by deferring to the men in these roles.

Variations

1. The board lengths and riverbed distances given are obviously not based on the team's size in terms of numbers and physical bulk or their effectiveness in working together. As you become familiar with this activity you will be able to gauge what board lengths and riverbed distances are best suited to an effective challenge.

2. A basic variation is to provide just two planks and have the squirrels quickly gobble up all but three sausages. You can then establish the time limit by announcing that the squirrels are all full and will not be hungry again for a specified number of minutes.

52

Blind and Mute Geometry

Summary Two teams wearing blindfolds try to form a square within a square using two lengths of rope. Occasionally a participant gains sight for a few minutes while simultaneously losing speech.

Objectives To explore teamwork and communication within and between teams, decision making, creative problem solving, evaluation, and quality.

Materials

1. Two lengths of 1/2 inch or larger utility rope with a soft sheath cover. One length should be shorter than the other; approximate lengths are 65–100 feet and 100–165 feet.

2. More than enough large, clean bandannas in a variety of colors and designs for all the participants. Fold the bandannas diagonally to facilitate their use as blindfolds.

Time Limit 35–60 minutes.

Procedure

1. Select an open area that has good footing and is free from obstructions.

2. Explain to the group that they will be experiencing an activity called "Blind and Mute Geometry" which is designed to help them experience and examine the concepts of teamwork and communication within and between teams.

3. Pass around the bandannas and ask each participant to take one. Explain that the blindfolds are optional accessories and note that no one will be made fun of or in any way deliberately tricked or embarrassed while blindfolded. Tell participants that peeking is a matter of challenge by choice. If they do peek, they should do so in an inconspicuous manner that will not make the accomplishment of the team's task easier. They are on their honor.

4. Keep the ropes out of sight in a bag or elsewhere. Bring the group to the area you have selected and divide them into two approximately equal teams of 5–7 members. Ask for volunteer observers provided that at least five members will remain in each team.

5. Inform each team of the following:

"You are stranded on a remote planet and need to send a message to the nearest space station before a disease you have contracted kills you all. The space sickness produces blindness. Occasionally sight is regained while speech is simultaneously lost. These sight-speech switches last a few minutes and are indicative of impending death. Your goal is to create out of two pieces of cord a structure that looks like one square centered within another square. If you create relatively true squares, and the space between the sides of each square is approximately 3 feet, the cords will function as a transmitter which you can use to send for help."

6. Give each team a drawing of one square centered within another square and tell them they have one minute before they must stand in teams wearing their blindfolds.

7. At the end of the minute retrieve the drawings and place a coiled rope a short distance from each group. As you drop each rope tell the group "Your cord is here." Inform them that given how long it will take a rescue team to get to them, they have 20-30 minutes to signal for help before the effects of their illness become deadly. Fudge the time factor if you have extra time and participants appear close to a solution. Medicine is not that precise a science.

8. From time to time tap a participant on the shoulder and tell the person he/she has sight but no speech. You can do this randomly or purposefully in terms of assisting the group if they are stuck or silencing a vocal leader. Allow the speechless participant 2–4 minutes before they switch back to blindness again. You can have more than one person sighted at a time on the same and/or different teams.

9. When the participants are satisfied that the transmitter is complete, tell them to take off their blindfolds and examine it. Ask them to lower it in place to the ground. Ask the observers and each participant to rate each square and the relationship between the two squares on a scale of 1-10 with ten being perfect. Doing this on a piece of scrap paper produces less biased results. Add the scores and divide by the number of entries to get an average score. If the score is over eight, they are able to send a message for help.

10. Conduct a review and discussion.

Commentary

This activity can be slow-paced and frustrating for some teams and should not be used in cold weather. However, it raises many communication, decision-making, planning, and organizational issues at a number of levels. Things to watch for include: whether they plan for a means of obtaining information from the mute person; how they decide which team has the small square and which has the large square; how they decide when they have finished; what communication systems are used within teams and how they communicate between teams; to what degree they function as one team given the fact that they have a common goal.

Variation

The basic way to vary the exercise is to change the shapes to concentric circles, or to equilateral triangles or rectangles that are twice as long as they are wide. One team can make one shape with no stipulation as to size (for example, "Make a square"). This highlights how resources, even excess resources, can complicate matters and block more creative, elegant, and efficient solutions.

53

Toxic Sludge Mobile

Summary   A team of scientists must determine how to make use of a "Toxic Sludge Mobile" in order to prevent toxic sludge from wreaking havoc and destruction on the surrounding population and environment.

Objectives   To explore teamwork, planning, and creative problem solving.

Materials
1. Two sturdy 4 x 4 inch beams 10 feet long.

2. A 33- foot length of clothesline that is soft to the touch. Do not use stiff plastic rope.

3. Two 10- foot boundary ropes.

4. A pair of scissors.

Time Limit   45–70 minutes, depending on how long the group plans.

Procedure
1. Locate a naturally low, muddy area or one that you can hose down so that it is quite soft and wet. The more trees, bushes, and boulders that are in the way the better. Ideally the team has to maneuver around and between natural or artificial obstacles (for example, picnic benches and/or tables) in order to get across the mud.

2. Place the two boundary ropes 33–66 feet apart.

3. Place the two beams, the rope, and the scissors outside the starting line.

4. Bring a team of 7–10 participants to the starting point. Use observers if the group is larger than ten.

5. Give the team the following instructions and then indicate that the exercise is underway:

   "An earthquake has burst open a huge vat of toxic sludge that was stored in your secret government laboratory. You are a team of scientists who must all reach the manual back-up controls which can open a hidden moat. The moat was secretly installed around the perimeter of the laboratory to catch any toxic sludge that might otherwise escape and wreak havoc and devastation on the surrounding population and environment. There is a sea of toxic sludge between you, the control panel, and the safety of higher ground. Behind you in the distance the sludge is rapidly rising and will soon be upon you.

"You have just unpacked the Toxic Sludge Mobile that was designed to be used to cross over the sludge manually in an emergency. The accompanying information indicates that:

- The cords and beams are chemically coated so that they are impervious to the sludge and you can touch them without fear of contamination.

- The sludge will rapidly penetrate and dissolve any other substances.

- Contact with humans leads to a certain and horrible death.

- The Toxic Sludge Mobile will dissolve and sink after 15 minutes of exposure on the sludge.

   Unfortunately, the instructions on how to use the Toxic Sludge Mobile were not included when it was boxed."

6. When the participants have succeeded or the 15 minutes on the sludge is up, conduct a review and discussion.

Commentary

This exercise illustrates the importance of planning, creativity, and trial-and-error use of a prototype. Participants should test various ways of moving on the beams on solid ground. There are several ways to maneuver the "Toxic Sludge Mobile." Do they creatively test different ideas or quickly seize on one that works and begin? Choosing a solution that takes more than 15 minutes, or is unstable enough to cause someone to fall off, leads to death by contamination.

   This activity can be used with **Earthquake I** (game 54) and **Earthquake II** (game 55) given their shared scenarios.

Variations

1. Give participants more rope.

2. Remove the 33- foot rope and scissors and instead tie four 8- foot ropes approximately 6 inches from the ends of each beam. Use a square or granny knot near the middle of the rope so that there are two approximately equal rope-tails which can be used as handles to move the beam. These handles should be on both ends of both beams.

3. Evenly space as many rope handles across the beams as there are team members. This approach tends to force a co-ordinated walk with all the left feet on one beam and all the right feet on the other. The choice of this solution illustrates how structure (for example, eight rope strands and eight team members) can block the creative search for other and perhaps better solutions.

54

Earthquake I

Summary   A team of scientists must determine how to bridge toxic sludge in order to prevent it from wreaking havoc and destruction on the surrounding population and environment.

Objectives   To explore teamwork, creative problem solving, and planning.

Materials

1. Eight bricks.

2. Four sturdy planks that are 10 feet by 2 inches by 12 inches. Substitute three 10 foot by 4 inch by 4 inch beams for teams with a lot of heavy members and/or more than ten members.

3. A 13- foot length of 1/3 inch rope or tubular webbing.

4. Two 13- foot boundary ropes.

Time Limit   50–70 minutes.

Procedure

1. Find a naturally wet and muddy area or create one by hosing one down.

2. Place the bricks and boundary rope as indicated in Figure 12 on the next page.

3. Brick placement is critical. Test the setup by making sure that the four planks can be walked on when placed as indicated in Figure 12. Also make sure none of the diagonals can be reached with a plank except the starred (*) one. Place a plank on the starred diagonal and walk on it to be sure it is stable.

4. Bring the group to the start. Observers are optional unless you have a large group in terms of numbers or total weight.

5. Give participants the following instructions:

   "You are a team of scientists. An earthquake has burst open a huge vat of toxic sludge which was stored in your secret government laboratory. Before you are the remains of a bridge that was designed to evacuate you safely in the event of a disaster. There is a sea of toxic sludge between you and the safety of higher ground which the bridge was designed to access. The eight block stanchions were specially made to resist the dissolving action of the sludge. The planking that was once a part of the bridge's walkway is splash resistant. Each plank can withstand one immersion in the sludge lasting 2–3 seconds before it loses its weight-bearing capacity. The sludge will rapidly penetrate and dissolve all other substances. Contact with humans leads to a certain and horrible death. Behind you, the sludge is rapidly rising and will soon be upon you."

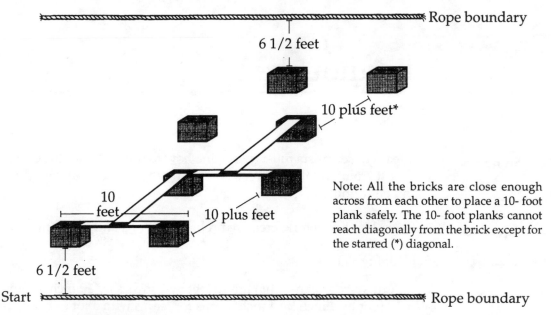

Rope boundary

6 1/2 feet

10 plus feet*

10 feet

10 plus feet

Note: All the bricks are close enough across from each other to place a 10- foot plank safely. The 10- foot planks cannot reach diagonally from the brick except for the starred (*) diagonal.

6 1/2 feet

Start — Rope boundary

Figure 12. Earthquake I: Setup.

6. Tell participants they have 20-30 minutes before the sludge rises to their level.

7. Once they have succeeded or the time is up, conduct a review and discuss.

Commentary

This is a challenging activity in terms of both finding a solution and implementation. The three-plank variation is quite difficult to execute and warrants three contacts with the sludge before each plank becomes dysfunctional. Failure to measure the distance of the starred (*) diagonal is typical and can often cost the amount of time needed to beat the deadline. This oversight exemplifies the tendency to block creativity based on the assumption that the future will be like the past. It is an error that is often made in order to save time and ironically it wastes time. The persistence of this tendency is remarkable. After just a few past confirmations that the plank is too short, teams tend to assume that it will continue to be too short in the future rather than take the time to test their assumption.

This activity often brings out sexism in which the males do all the lifting and leading. Some women apparently collude with the men in this process by deferring to the men in these roles. The activity can be used with **Toxic Sludge Mobile** (game 53) and **Earthquake II** (game 55) given their shared scenarios.

Variation   The basic variation involves using three 10 foot by 4 inch by 4 inch beams to make the challenge harder. Omitting the shorter starred (*) diagonal distance between blocks also adds to the level of difficulty.

55

Earthquake II

Summary A team of scientists must cross a moat of toxic sludge to escape their laboratory complex before the slime rises to their level and kills them.

Objectives To explore teamwork and creative problem solving.

Materials 1. Two 100- foot lengths of boundary rope.

2. Two planks, one longer than the other. Ideally, the longer plank should be a 10 foot by 4 inch by 4 inch beam. However, use whatever plank widths and lengths you have available as long as they conform to the setup requirements described in Procedure 1.

3. A 16–20 length of 3 1/2 inch rope or tubular webbing.

Time Limit Approximately 30 minutes.

Procedure 1. See Figure 13 on the next page for the setup of the activity. Position the two ropes to create the moat as shown in Figure 13. The moat is wider than either of the two boards. The solution involves putting the shorter board across the corner of the moat. It should just span the corner. The other plank must be long enough to reach the other side of the moat when placed on the middle of the first plank.

2. Bring the group to the site and give them the following information:

"You are a team of scientists. An earthquake has burst open a huge vat of toxic sludge that was stored in your secret government laboratory. Before you is the moat that was installed around the perimeter of the laboratory to catch any toxic sludge that might otherwise escape and wreak havoc and devastation on the surrounding population and environment. The moat cannot contain the volume of sludge released by the earthquake. It is about 3 feet below ground level and rising at a rate that will bring it upon you soon. To escape a horrible fate you must cross the moat before it overflows. The only materials you have to bridge the moat are the two planks and the rope. The sludge will rapidly penetrate and dissolve both planks and rope. If the toxic sludge contacts humans it leads to a certain and horrible death."

151

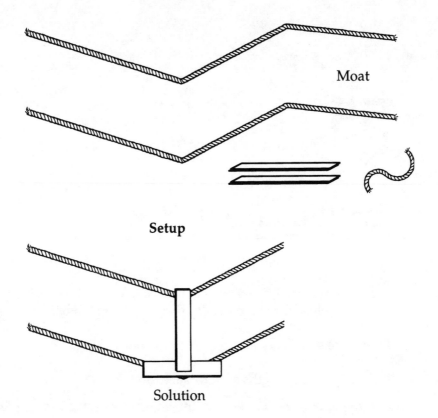

Moat

Setup

Solution

Figure 13. Earthquake II: Setup

3. Tell participants they have 10–15 minutes before the sludge rises to their level.

4. When they have succeeded or the time is up, conduct a review and discussion.

Commentary
This is a challenging activity which often demonstrates how time pressure can stimulate creative solutions. It can be used with **Toxic Sludge Mobile** (game 53) and **Earthquake I** (game 54) given their shared scenarios.

Variations
1. Use bricks intermittently spaced to create a more realistic moat to cross. The moat can also be made from 2 by 4 inch boards.

2. Vary the activity by varying the plank sizes. Use of a 13 foot by 4 inch by 4 inch beam makes for a very challenging activity, especially if the moat is made from bricks.

3. You can add another non-passable bend in the moat.

56

Nuclear Reactor I

Summary

Two or more teams of 3–5 compete for a contract to remove radioactive material from a nuclear reactor. The winner is the first team to discover how to move the materials from an explosive configuration to a safe one in the fewest moves.

Objectives

To explore creative problem solving and teamwork.

Materials

1. For each team, six canisters 7 inches high and 6 inches in diameter with one lid removed.

2. Three small balloons filled with water for each team.

Time Limit

30-40 minutes.

Procedure

1. With the participants out of earshot, set up the canisters and balloons for each team as follows. Place the six canisters in a row. Put the three water balloons (WB) in the third, fourth, and fifth canisters so that the first two canisters on the left and the one on the extreme right are empty (E). The configuration should look like this: E E WB WB WB E.

2. Divide the group into approximately equal teams of 3–5.

3. Assign each team to their site and give them the following instructions:

   "You are hazardous-waste removers who are competing for a contract with a company that operates nuclear reactors. Your task is to remove the nuclear byproducts in three of the canisters before you. In order to remove this material the pattern of empty and full canisters needs to be alternating in such a way that there is an empty (E) canister between each of those containing nuclear waste (W). The goal pattern would be either E W E W E W or W E W E W E and the space between the canisters must be approximately the same as it is now. Given the danger and expense of moving the canisters, the team who rearranges the canisters in the fewest moves will win the contract. The waste is wrapped in protective seals to allow you to experiment and use trial and error in relative safety. However, if you touch the seal or it breaks while you are moving a canister, you will automatically lose the contract and be taken to the nearest emergency room for decontamination and medical attention. As soon as you are ready to demonstrate your method, notify the facilitator. You are allowed to demonstrate just one method. In the event of a tie, the first team to demonstrate the fewest moves will win. You have all the information you need."

4. If time is limited, set a time limit of 10–20 minutes. When the teams have made their demonstrations or time is up, demonstrate the one-move solution if no team used it. This solution involves picking up the fourth canister, which is third from the right, and gently dumping its contents into the first or empty canister on the far left.

5. Conduct a review and discussion.

Commentary

This exercise quickly demonstrates how assumed rules can limit creative problem solving. It also highlights risk-taking issues. Some teams think of the solution but let the danger of bursting the balloon inhibit and even dissuade them from using it. Do teams spy on each other? Why or why not? Does a team using the one-move solution test it first? Why or why not?

This activity works well with **Flight** (game 48) and/or **Ringer** (game 49) as long as you do not use them too close to one another. It can be used consecutively or simultaneously with **Nuclear Reactor II** (game 57), which is a companion exercise.

Variations

1. Place balloons in the first three canisters and leave the next three empty.

2. For an impromptu presentation, use glasses half-filled with water and ad lib the scenario.

57

Nuclear Reactor II

Summary   Two or more teams of 3–5 compete for a contract to remove radioactive rods from a nuclear reactor. The winner is the first team to find out how to move the rods from an explosive configuration to a safe one in the fewest moves.

Objectives   To explore creative problem solving and teamwork.

Materials   Fifteen hardwood dowels, 3 feet by 1/8 – 1/4 inch for each team. Thin metal rods can be substituted.

Time Limit   20–30 minutes.

Procedure

1. Set up the dowels in the pattern depicted in Figure 14 on the next page, one setup for each team. Place the team setups out of hearing distance from each other.

2. Divide the group into approximately equal teams of 3–5.

3. Assign each team to their site and give them a 10–15 minute time limit and the following instructions:

   "You are hazardous-waste removers who are competing for a contract with a company who operates nuclear reactors. Your task is to create a new, more stable pattern of rods in which there are just three squares. Given the danger and expense of moving the rods, the team who restructures them into three squares in the fewest moves wins the contract.

   "You may not move any of the rods until you are ready to demonstrate your method. When you are ready, notify the facilitator. You are allowed to demonstrate just one method. In the event of a tie the first team to demonstrate the fewest moves will win. You have all the information you need."

4. When the teams have made their demonstrations or the time is up, show them the two-move solution (see Figure 14) if no team used it.

5. Conduct a review and discussion.

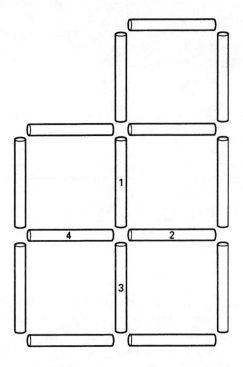

Figure 14. Nuclear Reactor II: Setup and Solution. (Solution: remove 1 and 2, or 2 and 3, or 3 and 4, or 4 and 1).

Commentary	This is a good exercise to show the relationship between creativity and looking at a problem from a different perspective. The presence of five small squares tends to dictate a small-square solution. Once the large square is seen, the two-move solution becomes obvious.

The exercise can be used consecutively or simultaneously with **Nuclear Reactor I** (game 56), which is a companion exercise.

Variations

1. If no group uses two moves, offer the following hints: The original position has six squares. There is a two-move solution.

2. You can begin with 12 rods that form a five-square pattern and ask participants to form two squares or give them the 12 rods and tell them to form exactly five squares by using them all.

58

Stevedores I

Summary   A team of stevedores has just unloaded seven barrels containing rare and fragile chemicals. The top of the manifest indicates the barrels must be stored in five rows with three barrels in each row.

Objectives   To explore teamwork, decision making, and creative problem solving.

Materials   Seven large metal or plastic barrels.

Time Limit   Approximately 30 minutes.

Procedure   1. Place the seven barrels together in a random pattern.

2. Bring the team to the site of the barrels and give them the following information:

   "You are a team of stevedores who has just unloaded these seven barrels containing rare and fragile chemicals. The top of the manifest indicates they must be stored in five rows with three barrels in each row. The bottom of the manifest which contained a schematic description of the storage pattern was ripped off and floated under the dock when you unloaded the barrels. A caution on the manifest indicates that failure to store the chemicals properly will lead to their deterioration. If you can't arrange them properly you will jeopardize your jobs and have to pay for the chemicals and any other losses entailed in the delay of their delivery. Time is of the essence."

3. Give participants a 15-minute time limit and tell them hints are available but cost time. The first clue costs one minute; the second, two minutes; and the third, three minutes. Offer the hints in the following order: (a) there are two horizontal rows; (b) there is only one vertical row; (c) there are two diagonal rows.

4. When they have succeeded or the time is up, conduct a review. Show participants the solution in Figure 15 on the next page if they didn't succeed.

This is a challenging activity for a team, which allows you to assess how well they entertain full and frank discussion versus dominance by a few when it comes to offering suggestions, deciding on the hint option, and moving the barrels. Use this game in conjunction with **Stevedores II** (game 59), which shares the same scenario.

Variation   The activity can be a competitive one in which teams of 3–5 members vie to be the first to complete the task.

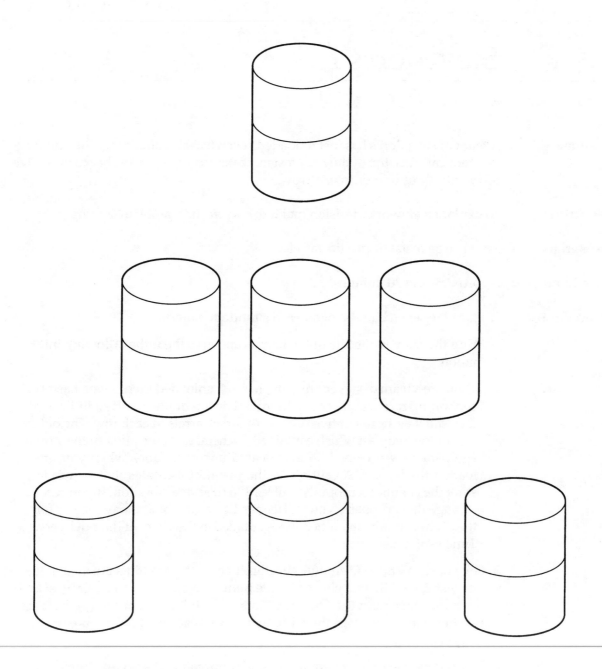

Figure 15. Stevedores I: Solution.

59

Stevedores II

Summary
A team of stevedores has just unloaded eight barrels containing expensive explosives. The top of the manifest indicates the barrels must be stored in two rows with five barrels in each row.

Objectives
To explore teamwork, decision making, and creative problem solving.

Materials
Eight large metal or plastic barrels.

Time Limit
Approximately 30 minutes.

Procedure
1. Place the eight barrels together in a random pattern.

2. Bring the team to the barrel site and give them the following information:

   "You are a team of stevedores who has just unloaded these barrels of expensive explosives. The manifest indicates that, unless the barrels are stored in two rows with five barrels in each row, they will explode in a matter of minutes. The bottom of the manifest which contained a schematic description of the storage pattern was ripped off and floated under the dock when you unloaded the barrels. If you can't arrange them properly you will jeopardize your jobs and have to pay for the explosives and any damage that their explosion causes. Time is of the essence."

3. Give participants a 15-minute time limit. If the team seems at a loss and you want them to succeed you can ask them if they want a hint that will cost them whatever time you choose to assign.

4. When the team has succeeded or the time is up, review and discuss. Show them the solution in Figure 16 on the next page if they didn't succeed.

Commentary
This is a challenging team activity that allows you to assess how well they entertain full and frank discussion versus dominance by a few when it comes to offering suggestions, deciding on the hint option, and moving the barrels. If you used **Stevedores I** (game 58) prior to this game, note whether and to what degree they improved in the above areas. Note that in terms of creativity, the solution to Stevedores I may have made solving this situation more difficult because it did not involve placing a barrel on top of another. This illustrates how past success can lead to failure when a different approach is needed to a

new problem. The same applies if you used this game first and followed it with **Stevedores I**.

Variation The activity can be competitive. Teams of 3–5 members vie to be the first to complete the task.

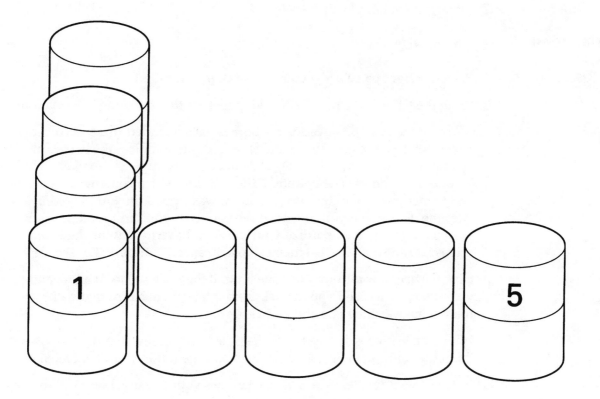

Place barrel 5 on top of barrel 1.

Figure 16. Stevedores II: Solution.

60

Jet Formation I

Summary   A team of jet pilots must arrange and then rearrange itself, moving a minimum number of pilots, to create a formation that points in the opposite direction.

Objectives   To explore teamwork, problem solving, and decision making.

Materials   None if you have a group of ten participants. For a group of less than ten, use a mat, a small piece of cardboard, or something similar to fill in spaces that would otherwise be occupied by participants.

Time Limit   Approximately 30 minutes.

Procedure   1. If your group is larger than ten ask for volunteers to be observers.

2. Tell participants they are a team of jet pilots flying in formation. Their first task is to organize themselves into a symmetrical formation that resembles that of a flock of geese. If there are fewer than ten participants, give them some type of markers or indicate where another jet would be.

3. When the group has achieved the correct formation tell them their goal is to reverse their direction by moving the *minimum* number of jets. Figure 17 on the next page shows the formation and the solution. Tell the group they may experiment with possible solutions. Note that they have 15 minutes before they must demonstrate their agreed upon solution.

4. When the group has demonstrated their solution, conduct a review. If you wish you can tell participants at some point that the solution involves just three moves. Showing them the solution, if they can't work it out themselves, is optional.

Commentary   This exercise engages everyone as their co-operation, in moving at least, is essential to achieving the task. The task illustrates the kind of problem which is more easily solved by one or two stepping outside the immediate situation to provide organization and direction. **Jet Formation II** (game 61) is a companion activity of greater difficulty that can be used after this exercise.

Variation   The task becomes more difficult and demands better communication if no practice is allowed. This option requires each jet to remain in formation and each move from one spot to another counts. Much more planning is needed and the inability to step away from the problem is a hindrance. Whichever option you use, refer to the other option during the review to illustrate that the nature of a problem often determines how best to solve it.

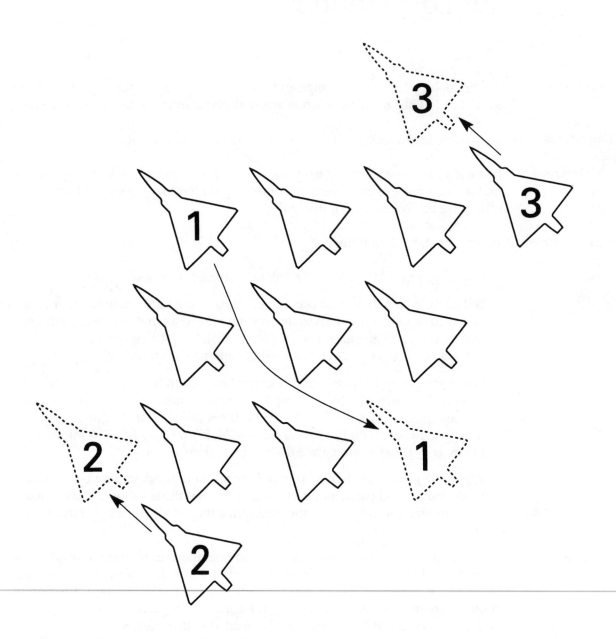

Figure 17. Jet Formation I: Formation and Solution.

61

Jet Formation II

Summary

A team of jet pilots must arrange itself into a formation that initially seems to require twice as many jets as they have available.

Objectives

To explore teamwork, problem solving, and decision making.

Materials

None if you have a group of ten participants. For a group of less than ten, use a mat, small piece of cardboard, or something similar to fill in spaces that would other wise be occupied by participants.

Time Limit

45–60 minutes.

Procedure

1. If your group is larger than ten ask for volunteers to be observers.

2. Tell participants they are a team of jet pilots who flies in exotic formations during air shows. Their goal is to organize themselves into a formation that is composed of five rows with four jets in each row. If there are fewer than ten participants, give them some type of markers or mats to indicate where another jet would be. Tell the group they have 20–30 minutes.

3. When they have achieved the correct formation or the time is up, have a discussion. Figure 18 on the next page shows the formation solution. You may decide to ask participants if they would like a hint. If they would, tell them that the formation looks like a common figure. The word "star" is a very helpful clue. Showing them the solution if they can't get it themselves is optional.

Commentary

This exercise engages everyone as their co-operation, in moving at least, is essential to achieving the task. It is a difficult challenge which usually requires full participation to be solved. **Jet Formation I** (game 60) is a companion activity of less difficulty and can be used before this one. If the team failed at this exercise use **Jet Formation I** after it if you think participants will benefit from a success with a related problem.

Variations

Give two teams of 3–5 members ten mats or hula hoops™ and have them compete to see who can achieve the formation first.

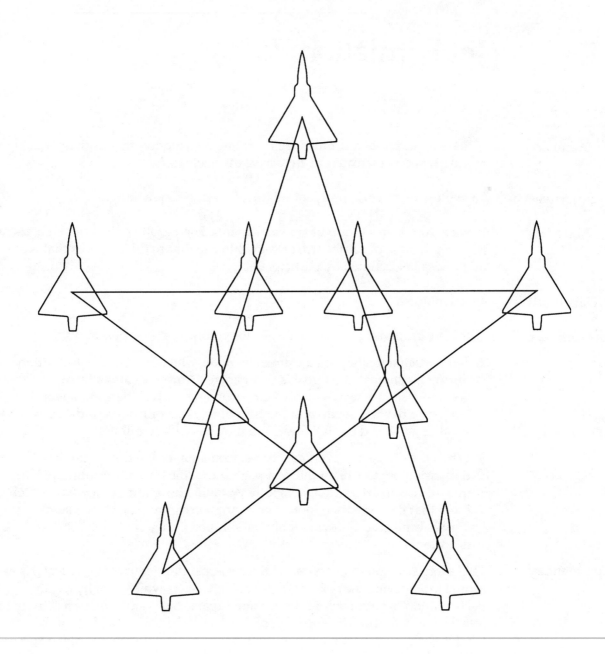

Figure 18. Jet Formation II: Solution.

62

Ostrich Eggs

Summary   Teams of biologists who are competing for a large grant must demonstrate their creative money-saving ability by isolating five ostrich eggs into separate cells using a minimum number of partitions.

Objectives   To explore teamwork and creative problem solving.

Materials   1. A large private parking area.

2. A piece of chalk for each participant plus some extras. Thick playground chalk is ideal.

Time Limit   30–40 minutes.

Procedure   1. Using chalk, reproduce Figure 19 on the next page on an asphalt parking area. Draw one diagram for each team, far enough apart to keep the teams out of earshot of each other.

2. Divide the group into teams of 3–5 members.

3. Give each group an instruction sheet (see Handout 62.1) and send them to their respective areas.

4. Do not answer questions that might help participants with a solution.

5. When all the teams have presented solutions or the time is up, determine a winner and conduct a review and discussion. If a three-line solution wasn't used, demonstrate the one in Figure 19.

Commentary   This game challenges a team's creative problem-solving ability. The activity works well as a lead-in to **Bring 'Em Back Alive!** (game 63), as it illustrates how past successes can block creativity by blinding a team to the use of different approaches which are more suitable to a new problem.

Variation   1. If you have a sand or gravel surface use sticks to draw the lines.

2. The activity can also be carried out by one team.

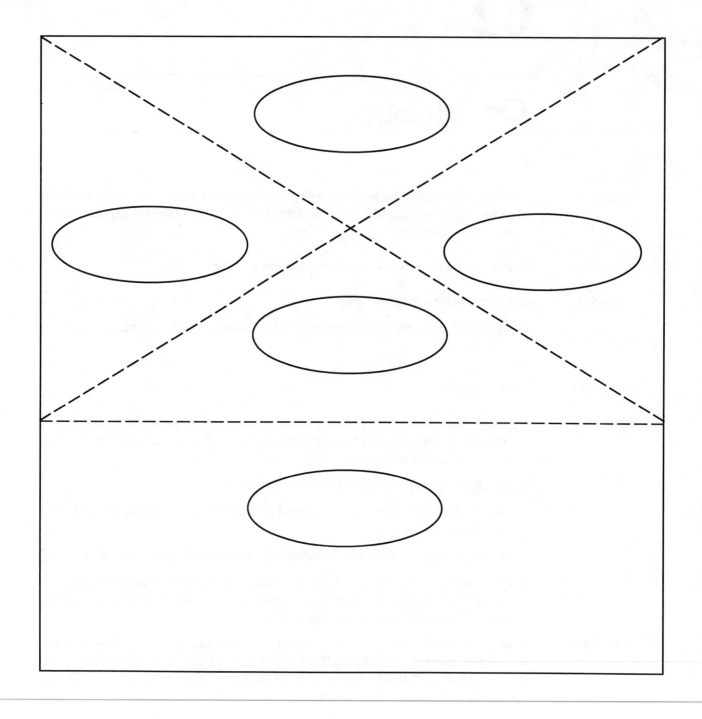

Figure 19. Ostrich Eggs: Setup and Solution.

Instructions

You are teams of biologists who are competing for a large grant. To win the grant you must demonstrate your creative money-saving ability by isolating five ostrich eggs into separate cells using a minimum number of expensive partitions. Each straight line chalk-mark represents a single partition. If there is a tie, the first team to use the fewest straight-line partitions will win the grant.

You have all the information you need. When you are satisfied with your solution show it to the facilitator. No solutions will be accepted once the eggs hatch in 15 minutes.

63

Bring 'Em Back Alive!

Summary
Teams of adventurers are competing for the prestigious "Bring 'Em Back Alive" cup. Each team has captured nine rare snakes. The coveted cup will be awarded to the team who can isolate the nine reptiles in separate pens using the fewest sections of "electric fence."

Objectives
To explore teamwork, communication, and creative problem solving.

Materials
1. A large, private, asphalt parking area.

2. A piece of chalk for each participant plus some spares. Thick playground chalk is ideal.

Time Limit
30–45 minutes.

Procedure
1. Using chalk, reproduce Figure 20 on the next page on the parking area for each team. Make sure that the teams will be out of earshot of each other.

2. Divide the group into teams of 2–3 members.

3. Give each team a procedure sheet (see Handout 63.1) and send the teams to their respective areas.

4. Do not answer questions about what constitutes a line or any others that might help participants to find a solution.

5. When they have all presented solutions or the time is up, determine a winner and review and discuss the exercise. If a one-line solution was not used, demonstrate the one in Figure 20.

Commentary
This game challenges creativity while demonstrating how written communication needs clarification as even simple words like "line" can be ambiguous. It also shows how assumed rules and fear of making a mistake can inhibit creativity.

This activity works well as a follow-up to **Ostrich Eggs** (game 62) to illustrate how past successes can block creativity by blinding a team to the use of different approaches which are more suited to a new problem.

Variations
1. If you have a sand or gravel surface use sticks to draw the lines.

2. This activity can be carried out by one team.

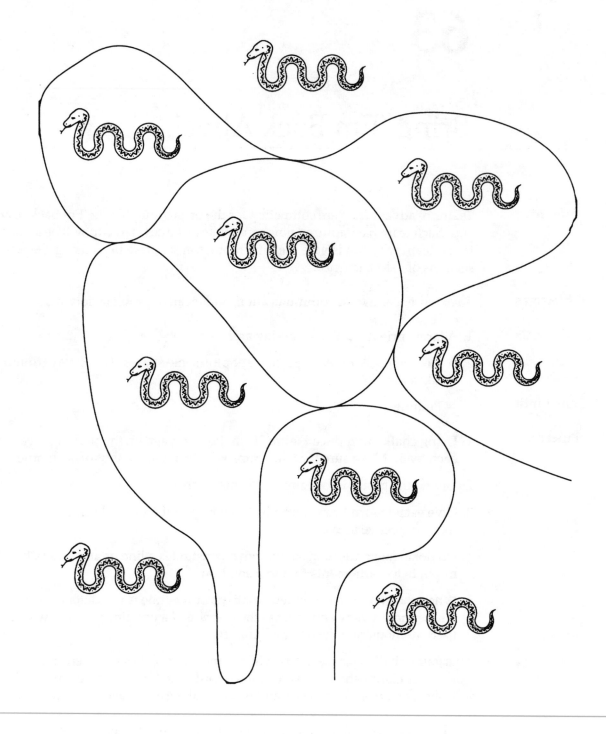

Figure 20. Bring 'Em Back Alive: Setup and Solution.

Instructions

You are teams of adventurers competing for the prestigious "Bring 'Em Back Alive" cup. You each captured nine rare snakes. The coveted cup will be awarded to the team who can isolate the nine reptiles in separate pens using the fewest chalk-lines of "electric fencing." In the event of a tie the first team to use the fewest lines of electric fencing will be the winner.

You have all the information you need. When you are satisifed with your solution, show it to the facilitator. No solutions will be accepted after 15 minutes have elapsed.

References and Further Reading

Consalvo, C. M. (1992), *WorkPlay*, King of Prussia, Pennsylvania: Organization Design and Development.

Consalvo, C. M. (1993), *Training with Outdoor Activities*, Aldershot, Hampshire: Connaught Training, Ltd.

Orlick, T. (1978), *The Cooperative Sports & Games Book*, New York: Pantheon Books.

Orlick, T. (1982), *The Second Cooperative Sports & Games Book*, New York: Pantheon Books.

Rohnke, K. E. (1991), *The Bottomless Baggie*, Dubuque, Iowa: Kendall/Hunt Publishing Company.

Rohnke, K. E. (1988), *The Bottomless Bag*, Hamilton, Massachusetts: Karl E. Rohnke.

Rohnke, K. E. (1984), *Silver Bullets*, Dubuque, Iowa: Kendall/Hunt Publishing Company.

Rohnke, K. E. (1977), *Cowstails & Cobras*, Hamilton, Massachusetts: Project Adventure.

Vecchione, G. (1992), *World's Best Outdoor Games*, New York: Sterling Publishing Co.

Weinstein, M. and Goodman, J. (1980), *Playfair*, San Luis Obispo, California: Impact Publishers. (Available from: The Humor Project, 110 Spring St., Saratoga Springs, NY. Telephone (518) 587-8770.)

Index of Games by Objectives

Most of the games in this book can be adapted to suit a variety of learning objectives. The following index lists the games that correspond to the learning objectives.

Objective	Title of Game	Page	Time Limit

About the Author

Carmine Consalvo, EdD, is the director of WORKPLAY, which he founded in 1984 to train professionals in the importance of humor, creativity, paradox, teamwork, and experiential training. His clients include a wide variety of organizations from both public and private sectors. Dr. Consalvo has written numerous articles on the role of humor in enhancing learning and productivity, and is the author of *Training with Outdoor Activities* (published by Connaught Training). He has taught at the University of Vermont's School of Education for many years.